HIDDEN TREASURES

FINDING THE MISSING REVENUE
IN YOUR DENTAL PRACTICE

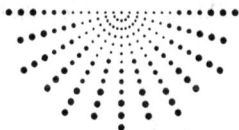

HEIDI MOUNT

KWE PUBLISHING, LLC

Mount, Heidi. *Hidden Treasures: Finding the Missing Revenue in Your Dental Practice*

ISBN (hardback): 978-1-950306-73-2

ISBN (ebook): 978-1-950306-74-9

Library of Congress Catalog Number: 2021910431

You can find Heidi at: CoachHeidiMount.com or scan the QR code below:

Pelagic Magic™ is a registered trademark of Jack's Diving Locker. The author has used it here with permission.

Cover design by Michelle Fairbanks, Fresh Design, mfairbanks.carbonmade.com.

Published by KWE Publishing: www.kwepub.com

CONTENTS

To my dad, who taught me to sail. Now, he's the wind beneath my wings; he taught me how to fly through the storm and soar. He always believed I could accomplish anything at all, showed me how to troubleshoot and problem-solve, led me to trust in the Lord, and taught me about life skills that help me succeed. He modeled early on how to serve others and show love.

I pray that out of his glorious riches he may strengthen you with power through his Spirit in your inner being, so that Christ may dwell in your hearts through faith. And I pray that you,
being rooted and established in love.
Ephesians 3:16-17

As I completed my book, my last boss and dear friend, Dr. Laura Marcoullier, breathed her last breath on March 2ⁿᵈ, 2021. As someone younger than me, loved by so many, she should have lived so much longer. I worked for her for thirteen years and poured my heart and soul into building her dental practice, serving her, laughing with her, and giving her my best effort. While she treated me especially well, she loved all of her patients and all of her team. We had so many wonderful memories—traveling, team bonding, and private girl chats. She will be truly missed. Thank you for all your encouragement, support, and for teaching all of us how precious every day is. Love you and miss you lots.

FOREWORD

By Ronald F. Arndt, DDS, MBA, MAGD
Master & Board-Certified Dental Coach

The legendary motivational speaker, Earl Nightingale, years ago, shared a true story with an ageless moral. The story was about an African farmer who was single-mindedly driven by a quest to find and own diamonds. These rare and valuable stones had been discovered, in large quantities, throughout the continent. Being so propelled in his desire to unearth millions of dollars' worth of diamonds, he sold his farm and set off to hunt for his treasure. For years, he wandered over the continent in search of his diamonds. After years of searching, and now broke, despondent, and unsuccessful in his quest, he threw himself into the river and drowned. Unfortunately, for the original farm owner, the new owner of his farm discovered, on his property, an unusual-looking, egg-sized rock that turned out to be among one of the largest diamonds ever found. Not only was the farm covered with these diamonds, but it also became the richest diamond mine the world has ever known. The original farm owner, undiscovered by him at the time, was the owner of his own "acres of diamonds," until he chose to sell his farm.

Why this message now? Because, in reality, each of us has the opportunity to identify our own "acre of diamonds," if only we take the time to realize that in our own practices, in our own backyards, we have a field of diamonds worth a fortune. We simply need to harvest what is there rather than running frantically for another 'dental magic pill.'

That is what Heidi's book *Hidden Treasures: Finding the Missing Revenue in Your Dental Practice* is all about: helping you identify the rough-cut diamonds in your backyard. With her support, you can polish them to a luster you could never have thought possible. Within these pages, you will find a trove of diamonds for you to harvest in your dental practice.

On a more personal note, at age forty-one, and fifteen years into dental practice, I had a heart attack. Though it nearly killed me, I viewed the heart attack as a gift. I had been running as fast as I could, trying to please my patients, my family, my banker, my own inner voice that drove me to work, work, work. I always, *always* compared myself to other people, struggling to be better than the other person. I had to be successful. I had to be the best. I was impatient and demanding because I was single-minded in my quest to get ahead as quickly as possible. Back then, I was striving to be successful according to how other people defined success. I wasn't striving to be happy on my own terms. Does any element of this resonate with you?

My story, not as rare as you might think, was about how a young dentist and businessman started his practice, made just about every mistake possible, and survived a life-changing, stress-induced heart attack. In retrospect, I wished I had the benefit of a dental coach. What I want for you is to *not* wait for a major health trauma, or a failed relationship, or any other kind of trauma to encourage you to make some shifts in your thinking that could potentially save your life. You don't have to be like me, you don't have to ignore all the signs and symptoms and wait for a near-tragedy to strike. What I want for you is to read, work, and learn with someone who can support you in developing and implementing steps that will enable you to take back control of your practice (*and your life*) rather than the practice controlling you.

If anything that I have shared thus far resonates with you, you know that it is important to get off that gerbil wheel. However, to do that, you must be willing and resolved to take action. You must have a desire for something different. You must want to vote for your life. It's the START that STOPS most of us. Consider working with an accountability partner like Heidi. Certainly, by reading *Hidden Treasures: Finding the Missing Revenue in Your Dental Practice* you can develop the mindset to create a new attitude. Her stories and anecdotes will masterfully guide you with her questions and insights to help you discover the beginning of the first day of a "new life." While I didn't say it was easy, the solution is rather simple: jump off the damn gerbil wheel. Over the following pages, Heidi will share with you some ideas that have worked for other doctors and teams, and they may work for you. What's beautiful about her process is that you get to decide the degree of change that you want for yourself. In my case, I chose massive and fast change. For you, it may be grabbing the low-hanging fruit and moving forward in a slow and methodical pace. It's your choice.

As Earl Nightingale said, "Opportunity doesn't come along, it is there all the time, we just need to see it." This is what *Hidden Treasures: Finding the Missing Revenue in Your Dental Practice* can do for you. This book can help you on your journey.

Heidi's insights, tools, and invaluable tips have the potential to help you create an extraordinary journey of reinvention that, **if applied**, will make you more money in less time while creating your exceptional life. Enjoy this journey as Heidi guides you to find your own "acre of diamonds" at the same time she helps you get off the gerbil wheel.

Ron

P.S. As a gift from a retired dental coach, I invite you to take the following assessment before you read this book and then reassess after reading the book. Then, compare your results. I suspect you will be pleasantly surprised.

How Do You Know If Your Business Is Killing You?

Take a moment right now and consider this checklist. Have you ever experienced any of these warning signs? Check off those that reverberate with you.

You find it difficult to get a good night's sleep because you are thinking or worrying about the business.

Your attention is on home when you are at work and on work when you are at home.

You tell your spouse that they are number one in your life when silently you are more focused on the success of your business. After all, it's who you are!

You act happy and content on the outside. In reality, your insides are churning and you never feel in control.

Your energy level begins to fade, and you make excuses when you know you have not been taking care of yourself. You pass it off as something else.

You are too busy to play those "goofy" games with your kids, who are so hungry for your attention.

You read the newspaper or business journals when your spouse is talking to you because you have so much to catch up on. Then, you fall asleep after twenty minutes because you needed "just a little nap."

On a weeklong vacation, it takes three to four days to unwind. You feel like a new person for one or two days, then the tension builds again, welling up uncontrollably, tightening every muscle. Sunday nights are the worst.

If you want something done right, you have to do it yourself. Only you can do it because it takes too much time to explain and delegate a task to another person.

You hear this voice in your head: "I don't need anyone else. I'm smart and can do it all on my own."

If you checked off a single one, consider it a red flag. Don't pass it off as inconsequential. The accumulation of these signs slowly and insidiously over time can be deadly.

PREFACE

Confidently, I bounded into the bustling office and plopped into the dentist chair. Why wouldn't I? I couldn't wait to see Dr. Robert. I adored our family dentist because he was always happy, and made me and my family feel warm and welcome. And digging into the treasure chest in his office, mounded with jumbo balls, super shiny objects, and other goodies was a highlight for me.

"Well, hello there, Heidi," Dr. Robert said.

I grinned. *"Hello!"*

If you know me, you won't be surprised to learn that I was a talkative kid. As I chatted with Dr. Robert, he asked, *"So, Heidi, what would you like to be when you grow up?"*

My eyes brightened and I sat a little straighter in the chair. Without hesitation, I almost shouted, *"A dentist!"*

I'm sure in the back of his mind, Dr. Robert was rolling his eyes! He was probably thinking, *Of course she said that! She's at the dentist!* As he made a note in my record, however, Dr. Robert just beamed at me.

For the next fifteen years, I could always count on seeing my favorite hygienist and of course, Dr. Robert, every six months for my checkups. I always liked the way the gloves they wore tasted like mint. The team in Dr. Robert's office always made me feel special by asking me questions about my life and what I was interested in. When I visited them, I always felt like a superstar.

Right before my high school graduation in 1988, I happily greeted Dr. Robert as he approached my chair.

He shook his head as if wondering how so many years had passed. He said, *"Wow, what is next for you, young lady?"* When I shared that I was planning to go to college, he asked, *"What do you want to do as an adult?"*

Excitedly I exclaimed, *"I'm not sure yet if I'm going to become a dentist or a hygienist."*

Briefly, he paused, seeming surprised, and then picked up my chart and opened it.

"I just have to show you something." Pointing to my file, I looked down at his notes, and there it was from 1974: *'When I asked, Heidi said she wants to be a dentist.'*

I shook my head in slight disbelief, having forgotten my words from my childhood. Then, we both laughed, and my heart felt so warm. While I was amused, I was not surprised that I gave the same answer at age four that I did at age eighteen. I was drawn to dental offices because of Dr. Robert, my happy and trustworthy dentist who was always warm and welcoming to me.

Today, I have the career of my dreams as a dental coach, and I am living the life I always wanted. Dentistry today has more opportunities than ever before. Just like my hero, Dr. Robert, and his team, I want to help others, and now it is the dentists I am helping. With over three decades of experience, I love sharing my expertise! I truly treasure life and delight in helping others go after their dreams. My goal in writing and sharing this book with you is to enable you to design your best life.

1

BEING THE CAPTAIN
OF YOUR OWN SHIP!

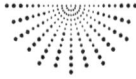

Deep Dark Water

A few years ago, my scuba diving buddies encouraged me to do a "black water dive" called Pelagic Magic©. The word pelagic means "nowhere near the land" or "the bottom of the sea."

Led by Jack's Diving Locker on Kona, the Big Island of Hawaii where I now live, black water diving is not just night diving, which is something many advanced scuba divers do. On night dives, scuba divers observe manta-rays, eels, crabs, and other creatures during the night. Black water diving is completely different.

Every evening, millions of sea creatures emerge from the bottom of the depths of the ocean. As glowing jellyfish, zooplankton, fish, and other deep-sea critters hunt for a meal and a mate, divers shine their lights at this incredible sight under the water. They attract microscopic zooplankton like moths to a porch light, which in turn draws in miniature open ocean predators like jellyfish and squid.

My friends kept raving about how amazing the dive was. *"You can flick your fins together and it looks like Fourth of July fireworks,"* one of them said.

Another chimed in and shared, *"You can totally see through some of the fish, and others are iridescent!"*

Their enthusiasm for this dive intrigued me.

However, going on this dive meant being in a boat at least a few miles away from the shore, over at least 5000 feet of water. Then, tethered underneath the boat, we would scuba dive about fifteen to forty-five feet down in dark black water. Try knowing what's up or down when you can't see your hand in front of your face! On top of that, my husband and I only had about twenty dives under our belt, so both of us thought this excursion sounded pretty darn scary!

I am a highly analytical person, so of course, I had to fully analyze the situation. My dive buddies are pretty smart people; I knew they would only suggest this adventure if they believed in me and knew that I could do it and that we would have a lot of fun. Logically, it made sense. With a lot of hesitation, my husband and I agreed to the dive.

When we were booking the reservation, one of the employees at Jack's Diving Locker said, *'Every trip is unique, so you can see something different on every dive.'*

I was told that some photographers take pictures and discover creatures that even scientists have never seen or identified before. That sealed the deal for me. Nervous or not...I was determined to go black water diving! After all, you only live once right? If I was going to die, I at least would have died doing something I love.

Jack's Diving Locker uses highly skilled dive masters, so their job is to guide us and keep people safe. I was thinking, *Yay!* **I have some-body who has confidently 'been there, done that'** and *promises to care for me.*

That night came. We brought our gear to the boat, they welcomed us, and we took a seat. After we had boated out a few miles, I was really starting to get nervous. I could barely see any shore and there was just a sliver of moon. During the day, the water is crystal-clear and bright blue. However, at night, I could barely see the light a few feet directly ahead of the boat. The captain started to explain that they would carefully place a parachute in the water and use it as a sea anchor. Basically, it was used to keep the boat from whipping us around the big deep blue. Gulp.

Then, the divemaster threw six ropes over the edge of the boat with weights tied to the end of them. These weights would tell us if we were at the end of our ropes. No pun intended! The ropes were spaced out around the boat: two off the bow, two off the stern, and two off the middle of the boat.

This is what was going through my head:

- *Which one of us will be the first to jump out of the boat into the black water?*
- *Will a big whale take us all out?*
- *Did some great white sharks hear the motor shut off and think we are fish bait?*
- *Will I freak out, forget my scuba diving skills, sink to the bottom, and never, ever be found?*
- *Am I capable or even experienced enough to handle an emergency?*
- *What if I can't do it?*
- *Basically, what the heck did I just get myself into?*

With each question going on in my head, I became more anxious. It was too late to back out at this point, so I geared up as slowly as possible. I donned my wetsuit, always an awkward wriggle. Then, I turned on my air and threw my scuba gear on my back.

This means I wear a buoyancy control device or BCD which is basically my life support system in a vest. The BCD has gauges that tell me how deep I am, the temperature of the water, if I am ascending or descending too fast, or if I have too much nitrogen in my body.

Like every good scuba diver, I've got inflators that make me neutrally buoyant, emergency releases to bring me back to the surface, a dive knife in case I need to bop a shark on their nose or knife my way out of a net or tangle, drain buttons to fill or vent air into my life support vest, and gauges to tell me how long or deep I have been diving. If my gear fails and I need to make it to the surface, I disconnect my valve and locate a little gizmo to blow air into my vest which will inflate it into my own personal life jacket.

My most important gear is the gauge that tells me how much air is left in my tank! Don't worry...if I run out, I can signal one of my dive buddies for their alternate source of air. The key is not to panic. As you can see, positive self-talk is a life necessity.

Keep in mind, I had to remember all of this in the pitch black while I was scared of the unknown.

On our boat, miles away from land, the divemaster started giving our black water dive instructions:

"All you have to do is hold a flashlight and look for tiny sea creatures. When you spot something, look at it and enjoy it. While you are staring at it, keep your light on it and make sure to share what you see with your diving buddies."

In other words, he explained that the creature would stay with your light, so we should keep the light on it, then move our flashlights to our left so we could keep passing it around for the other divers to enjoy.

By this time, I literally asked the divemaster, *"Um, do I have to go?"*

He said, *"Nope."*

All I could think was, *I can't waste the $175 bucks we paid for me to dive! And what if it is as awesome as my friends say? #FOMO*

Trying to look normal, I casually inquired, *"Is it common for people to back out?"*

Once again, he said, *"Nope."*

Being the only woman on the boat, I thought that he would comfort me with some divemaster cliché. Again, nope.

So, with a lump in my throat, I let him tether the rope to my BCD. Turning on a flashlight, he handed it to me and said, *"Whatever you do, don't drop it!"*

No pressure there!

This was it...in that instant I knew I had to make a final decision.

After properly attaching the wristband and holding the light, I turned slowly, looking out at nothing but pure black ocean. There was no land in sight, it was just dark water, me, and my gear. Of course, I went in last. Not seeing any other divers ahead of time, or knowing their thoughts while under the boat, I had to have faith to take the plunge. I took a big stride off the boat and plopped into the water with my fifty pounds of life-saving Rambo gear. Thank God I didn't sink because, with great customer service, Jack's Diving Locker made sure there was air in my BCD.

At this point, I was so freaked out that I was just trying to follow the basic skills of a scuba diver. The self-talk really kicked in:

"Come on, Heidi, you got this! What's the first step? It's to give the boat captain your 'okay' hand signal to let him know you are all good!"

I wanted to do the normal routine by putting my fist on my head to give the standard *"I'm okay"* scuba diving sign. For some reason, I couldn't! And it wasn't because I froze in eighty degree water or that I forgot. It was because as soon as I hit the water, my flashlight went out! I only had light for a split second. I felt extremely panicky and thought, *Seriously? Dead batteries! Why me?*

All the other divers were successfully under the boat and I felt alone. Hopelessly, I looked at the captain, wanting him to rescue me from being floating shark bait and hand me a towel.

Did he pull me out of the water and save me from this torture? Nope. He immediately swapped out the dead flashlight for a new flashlight and encouraged me to *"go down and have fun. You won't regret it!"*

Jumping in that black water was the scariest decision that I ever made.

How did I feel once I made it under the boat, saw the other lights, and joined in with the rest of the divers? Oh, my gosh guys, it was like an ADHD dream! There were so many out-of-this-world, colorful creatures that I never wanted to leave. My friends were right—I could flick my fins and see fireworks! There are very few places in the world where you can experience the beauty of bioluminescent water and the Big Island of Hawaii is one of them. It was the best experience I have ever had!

When I look back on that dive, one of the absolute best things I have ever done, I shake my head when I remember that I almost chickened out! I could have given in to my fear and never had the guts to attempt a Pelagic Magic© dive again. I would have always regretted not living my life to the fullest potential.

I share this tale because it is the perfect analogy for the decision you have before you. You can either keep doing what you're doing and have the same results, or you can have a positive mindset and use this book to choose to improve your life, become the captain of your own ship, and live the life you've always wanted.

It's entirely your choice.

There are a number of lessons I discovered from my Pelagic Magic© story:

- *There is always fear in the unknown.*
- *It takes a different mindset to level up.*
- *I had to take a leap of faith, even knowing I may not accomplish the goal the first time.*
- *I had to take a risk, and I was braver than I imagined.*
- *Even with the right equipment, we all need guidance and vision.*
- *We can all imagine the vision we want to achieve, but someone may need to show us the way.*
- *Making a decision to put fear aside and go after a goal, even knowing I may lose some money in the attempt.*
- *Earned bragging rights of accomplishing something so cool are amazing.*

There is Always Fear in the Unknown

Honestly, the Pelagic Magic© tour brought me face-to-face with terror. I was incredibly worried about sharks, being in the dark, swimming blindly, remembering all the scuba diving training, and doing something I had never tried.

It is normal for us to have a fear of the unknown. Fear is something all of us face at points in our lives. There are always decisions to make and plans to execute that can seem over your head, impossible to achieve, or too hard to accomplish alone. Some things in life seem overwhelming or unattainable.

I want you to consider where you are today in your dental practice. If you are far ashore from where you want to be, it's important to change course. Think about this: if doing what you are currently doing hasn't gotten you where you want to be in business, isn't it time to take some calculated action? Only when you are willing to take a leap of faith will you get to experience the highest level of rewards. As the saying goes, "Fortune favors the bold." And we are all stronger than we think.

Think about changes you have made in your life. Often, they are uncomfortable at first. So, what is the most common issue you notice? We fall back to old routines, right? Even if they aren't working for us anymore, the routines we are used to become comfortable. However, "comfortable" doesn't get results. The way to grow is to break out of your comfort zone and take an adventure. Trust me, you've got to get comfortable with being uncomfortable if you want anything more out of life!

It Takes a Different Mindset to Level Up

Before I went on the Pelagic Magic© dive, I had to adjust my mindset to be bold and to just do it. Unless we improve our mindsets we keep repeating the same non-eventful patterns. That's not how you get to where you want to be, right?

Our incredible brains have an amazing capability called neuroplasticity. Neuroplasticity is just a fancy way of saying our minds can adapt and change with experience. You may think only children have minds like sponges, ready to accept information, but adults have minds like this, too. Isn't it refreshing to know that we can also learn and adapt as adults? Our brains are a lot like computers, and they can be reprogrammed. It's great to know you always have the ability to adopt a different, better mindset.

Research shows with a fixed mindset, people believe they are born with what they have and cannot grow. However, with a growth mindset, people accept their neuroplasticity and realize that they can change. When they make these changes, their lives are impacted positively. Throughout this book, I will point to growth mindsets and encourage you to adopt a positive outlook, too.

My desire to write this book and share these topics is because I love helping dentists and their teams achieve their dreams. If I can do it, so can you! I want to teach you some important lessons by sharing what some of my clients went through. My goal is to prevent you from making the same mistakes and to help you make better decisions. Listen to some examples of some *'stinking thinking'* these dentists and employees had.

Old Mindsets That My Clients and Their Team Changed

- *"We have to verify the patients' insurance or they will leave!"*
- *"I don't do bonuses or they will expect it every month."*
- *"I can't tell the new patient they need four crowns or they will think we are trying to buy a new car."*
- *"Patients won't pay for an extra cleaning if the insurance doesn't cover it."*
- *"There is no point in having a team meeting because it's just a big complaint session."*
- *"I don't want to invest in my team because they don't stay long enough."*
- *"If we are not a preferred provider for insurance companies, the majority of our patients will leave."*
- *"Our patients can't afford treatment."*
- *"I get stuck with doing everything myself."*
- *"It's easier to do it myself so I know it's done right."*
- *"I can't raise my fees, people are out of work."*
- *"I feel like I am a lousy leader."*

How many of you have heard these types of examples or said them yourself? We probably all have at one point in our career.

Even With the Right Equipment, You Also Need Guidance and Vision

During the Pelagic Magic© dive, I could have probably just banged the flashlight to get it to work. However, I didn't think about that as a possible solution when I was feeling so anxious in the dark water. Sure, I had all of the equipment I needed for the tour. Without the divemaster's vision and expertise, I would have been discouraged and probably continued doing the same familiar dives. I probably would have climbed back up into the safety of the boat where I was comfortable or just quit, and I could have missed out on one of the best experiences in my life.

It's the same way that distractions can get in our heads and in the way of our goals or our dreams. As dentists, everyone has access to the same instruments, equipment, and resources. What makes the difference is how you use them.

I was grateful to have the great team at Jack's Diving Locker guiding and encouraging me on my excursion. Similarly, I will be here as your guide throughout this book. Through assessments in these chapters, I will help you determine where you currently are in your practice, and you can decide if you want to make some adjustments to improve your life. I will help you envision your own outcomes. Then, I will share with you my best processes so you can achieve your own dreams and goals.

In your life, you may want to achieve the best things ever, right? While I can't explain what "the best thing ever" means to you, I do know that if you don't trust and take risks then you may not experience the extraordinary.

In my years of experience as a dental coach, I've seen other dentists choke and stop short of heading for the destination they wanted. And our time here on earth is precious. It breaks my heart when I see dentists fall short of making landfall, which is their true potential.

You may be searching for answers and stop yourself because you ask:

- *What if it doesn't work or I can't do it on my own?*

I'm here as your divemaster to ask you in reply:

- *What if it does?*
- *What if all you need is a pro to show you the way?*

> **DO YOU WANT TO BE THE CAPTAIN OF YOUR OWN SHIP?**
>
> Coach Heidi Mount

Do You Want to Be the Captain of Your Own Ship?

It is actually easier than you think. It is time to reboot your dental practice, shift your mindsets, and be more positive. Make a decision from this day forward to stop the negative, and take charge of your own ship. You can think of the ship as the six inches between your ears or taking charge of your life. Either way, these are ultimately your decisions.

Financially speaking, I'm here to tell you that for every year you wait and don't make a change, it costs most U.S. practices an average of $100,000 or more a year in lost revenue or profit.

Think about it: What could *you* do with an extra $100 grand a year?

While we know that money isn't everything, it can afford a better life for yourself, your team, and your family members. Financial freedom and the life you have always dreamed of are within your reach. You just have to decide:

- *Do you want to be a slave to your business, or would you rather be the captain of your own ship?*
- *If you are a member of a dental team, wouldn't you rather be a part of the crew actively helping the dentist steer the stern to reach the dream destination?*

Where Do You Begin?

Congratulations! Now that you've decided to be the captain of your own ship, where do you start? It's normal to feel confused about the beginning of your journey. Most dentists have so many decisions to make and projects to do that they don't know where to begin. They and their team feel overwhelmed, frustrated, and totally alone at sea. Can you relate to what I am saying, Doctor?

I have good news: life doesn't have to be so hard! Instead of helplessly drifting, you can take actions that get results! Every position on a boat has an important role that helps with the forward motion. It's best to have a grip on the helm of your business or else your business will have a grip on you!

Many of you are reading this and thinking, *How can I do anything more, Heidi? I'm overloaded with to-do lists. I've got too many decisions to make and so many projects to tackle that I don't even know where to start!*

Since something resonated with you to read this book, trust me, you are ready to take the helm and start making smart choices to steer your ship in the right direction. You may still be asking, *how?*

How do I:

- *Navigate to my goals?*
- *Get further faster?*
- *Find the treasure at the end of the map?*

The best part of starting with this book is that you now know that you do not have to run your business alone or unsupported. Just as I put my faith in the divemaster at the water's edge, you can put your faith in me.

When you stop focusing on the "what ifs" and throw out distractions, you get to enjoy amazing benefits you never imagined were possible and enjoy the life that you dreamed of becoming. Instead ask, *"What if it DOES work?"*

Every dentist and employee has a unique situation, a different personality, a diverse background, a particular skill level, and unique career goals. I don't believe in a cookie-cutter system or program. Throughout this book, I will share a handful of stories and situations from clients I've helped. Keeping in mind that your practice is unique, I encourage you to see if some of their concerns and issues are similar to yours. See if you recognize any early signs or symptoms that are currently going on in your dental practice.

Dr. Takeover Makeover (Acquisition)

What a challenge! I was contacted by a dentist who bought her practice from a gentleman who passed away suddenly. His loyal team of employees were nice yet had never received any official training. Patients came to him because he was the cheapest dentist in the state. And no wonder! All of their practice's patient information was in paper charts, they used an extremely old version of dental software, and they had lots of patients who weren't showing up for their dental appointments. There were many eye-raising issues, including patients who did financial arrangements on a handshake and the condition of their "old"/outdated building. While my client was excited to finally be a dental practice owner, she didn't know how to tackle these issues and develop a thriving business.

Imagine taking over a practice where the dentist is doing crowns for one-third of the normal fee, patients are distraught over the loss of their dentist and friend, and the entire team in disarray. Where would you begin? My client had a huge practice loan to pay, an office that desperately needed a facelift, patients with whom she needed to establish rapport and trust, computer software to program and update, a team in need of comfort and consolation, and a challenge to try to stay afloat with an astronomical amount of bills.

Working together, Dr. Takeover Makeover and I set goals and

prioritized all of the tasks to be accomplished. Our first goal was inspiring and motivating the team, of course. Once the team agreed to jump on board with the doctor's vision, they were excited to learn more and improve their skills. Next, fees were more than doubled to charge the fair market value, and the team members were fully trained in helping patients to value their dental practice and services. After, the office was nicely refurbished with new floors, equipment, and high-tech dental technology; the job descriptions were updated with full accountability, and improvements like an office manual, standard operating manuals, going chartless, and hygiene protocols were put in place. We began running the office with 70% overhead within six months. #MindsetChange

As we continue to work on a clear, well-written business plan, set goals, fine-tune systems, and train on the verbal skills to grow her practice, my client and her team get closer to living their true vision for their life. We keep working on long-term decisions that bring them more security and joy into their life.

Think of a moment when you may have felt like your dental practice needed a "practice makeover." Which areas would you like to improve? It is time to make that wish list and take action, because if nothing changes then nothing changes!

> **Don't wait for your feelings to change to take action;**
> **Take the actions and your feelings will change.**
> **—Barbara Baron**

Let's take a pause in this book. As you read, I encourage you to grab a journal as this is an interactive book. Jot down your answers to the exercises, and any questions or thoughts you have.

Seriously, I want you to get the most out of your investment and time with me today. Trust me on this assignment. I would like you to pull out the letter you received when you were accepted into dental school. Yes, put the book down and go find it. If you are married, grab your significant other and include them in this activity.

Now, read your acceptance letter out loud. Take a couple of minutes to think about your feelings when you first read that letter. What did you imagine things would be like after you graduated dental school, you got some letters after your name and you were finally called "*doctor*"?

When I opened my acceptance letter I felt...

After I became a doctor, I imagined my life would be described as...

Let's evaluate your life now. Be honest...did it turn out the way you imagined?

Why don't you write in your journal about your current situation and what results would you rather have instead?

When I went on the Pelagic Magic© dive, initially I greeted it with a great deal of enthusiasm because I had heard amazing things from my friends! They had experienced the dive firsthand and knew I needed to achieve this someday, too.

When one of my clients first contacted me, they had also heard great things that I had done for other dentists. They were definitely intrigued and wanted to hear how they could achieve more too.

They thought to themselves, *Hey, I'd like to have more time with my family and do the things I love to do! I'd like to make more money! I don't know what I don't know and want to know if I am missing something!* And, *Something needs to change because I can't keep doing this much longer.*

Now, I'd like to stop here for a second and share that money is not everything. Money is simply a means for exchange. Basically, people who make money have more time, more options, and more freedom.

Identify Who You Are and Allow Others to Help

As a dentist, you wear so many hats. When you make more money, you have the ability and freedom to remove several hats.

Wouldn't it be great to...

- *Pay for a house cleaner to keep your place clean while you go to the spa?*
- *Hire someone else to tackle your marketing, handle your accounting, manage your human resources department, wash your car, mow your lawn, do your grocery shopping, or use an application to monitor your supplies?*
- *Donate to your favorite non-profit or give more gifts?*
- *Contribute more to your retirement?*
- *Travel to all the places you've always wanted to see?*

Making more profit is about creating more options for yourself. It also gives you the ability to create a better life for you and your whole team.

Right now, you may have tired crew members. And there are days when you feel like you are drifting out to sea with no end in sight. Wouldn't you rather have smooth sailing and enjoy the trip? If you are on a dental team, wouldn't you like a happier, cohesive environment where everyone is rowing in the same direction? What if your dentist could share a percentage of the profit with you and the team? Would that improve your mood and create a fun atmosphere? Oh, yeah!

If you're feeling a little anxious reading this, that's a good thing. Whenever we decide to embark on an adventure, we feel a little excitement and a little anxiety. That's actually a great thing to feel because that nervousness is your body telling you that great things are coming! It's normal to feel some inner resistance; when you ask yourself, *"Do I have to change?"* you are feeling called to make a change for a reason and it's important to listen to your gut. And the best part about making an adjustment in your life is that you are not in it alone. I am here to guide and support you all the way through.

Sometimes when you hire help and work with a consultant, they provide a pile of checklists, scripts, and standard operating manuals that they give to every client or they tell you to do things that you notice didn't improve your business. Even when you own the materials, most offices have their binder tucked away in a drawer somewhere. This is like giving an old treasure map out...there is no more gold to be found. You can't use cookie-cutter systems or old-fashioned strategies and expect it to work in the modern world.

What I have to offer is a unique process. I climb aboard the ship with you, get with you on the helm, and talk about your unique needs. When you share your goals with me, I help you figure out the best way for you to steer to YOUR desired treasure.

Taking this leap with a trusted coach lessens the risks and enhances the opportunity for exciting new improvements. Similar to the Pelagic Magic© dive, you will have many useful instruments at your fingertips. Moreover, it takes an expert such as myself, someone who has "been there, done that" to show you the way.

I will be candid that making some improvements may feel strange at first. Just as I had to adjust to using a flashlight in pitch-black water, you may feel a little odd trying out better methods and other ways of thinking. Like any new skill, it will take a little time to master, and your results will be amazing. If you feel uneasy or unsure how to get there, I'm happy to be your compass and guide you back on course towards your true north.

I share with my clients:

By improving your mindset and taking action, you will create great habits, a positive environment for everyone, and a more consistent outcome.

All of us want the dream life of living happily ever after. Only you can decide what will truly make you happy. Even if you wanted to be married FOREVER, it will take work, a positive mindset and commitment. **I will be the first to say that empty talk achieves nothing.** Action takes investment and good intentions won't pay for anything. Your words must have value for people to listen.

Resistance: Even a Dead Fish Can Go with the Flow

By answering this call to sea, I challenge you to make a commitment. Initially, since you are adjusting your course and creating new habits, there may be some resistance.

That is normal.

It's hard to swim against the current if you don't know the most efficient way to paddle. The thought of making a change can be hard. It's been said that change itself is never painful, as it is the resistance to change that is painful. Upon your instruction, many employees will say things like, *"If we do that, patients will leave!"* or *"But we've always done it this way!"*

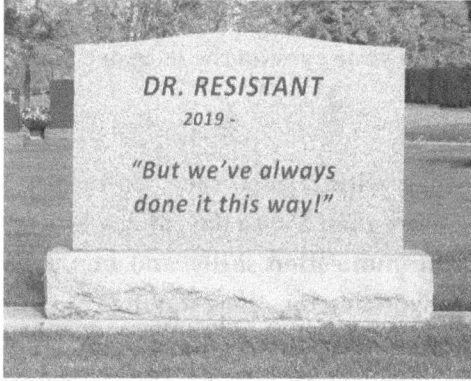

The interesting thing is…if every dentist does these easy steps that I will share, they can reach higher goals.

In other words, these things that work for a broke dentist are the same things that work for a successful dentist who wants to grow.

Challenges and Commitment

Fears…do you get scared? Do you stop part of the way? Do you hesitate? Do you procrastinate? Well, great, you passed the humanity test, and trust me, I did, too. By working together with me and taking that courageous step to move in a better direction, you will commit to achieving the better quality of life you desire. With your call to sea comes a commitment.

I want you to commit to:

- **Jot down your goals and share them with me: dive deep and understand what it is you really want. While many of my clients answer that they want more money, I challenge them to ask themselves, "why"?**

- **What will more money bring to you? Write your answers in your journal.**

- Keep calm and steady at the helm: while we are working together, keep your eyes on the treasure you will receive.

Often when I work with clients, they see results as soon as one day. They make more than $500 a day, plug a leak in their practice, improve their communication skills, and implement systems for more success. By working together, staying the course, having my eyes on your practice, keeping your goals in mind, and trusting that the process works, you will be able to access your hidden revenue and the treasures you and your team desire.

Are you willing to take the wheel and keep steady on your course? Are you willing to continue doing the work until you access your hidden treasure? Write your affirmation in your journal.

Staying the course: when my clients work with me and follow the steps I share, they experience success. When my clients "rock the boat" by falling back to their old habits, they fall behind where they could be.

Are you willing to adopt a growth mindset? Are you open to new ways of running your practice? Write your affirmation in your journal.

As you and I embark on this adventure together, I'll share my expertise and stories about helping other dentists navigate to their better life. I will analyze your unique needs and together we will collaborate to create a strategic plan. This plan, like a treasure map, will take you directly to the goals you want to achieve.

Ultimately, my goal for you is to feel empowered, excited, and energized by your dental practice! Stick with me, as I will not leave you feeling like you are drifting out to sea!

The clients with whom I have the best success are those who are highly motivated, dream big, surround themselves with positive people, take responsibility, and do what they love. Most importantly, they understand that a coach doesn't do it for them.

Team Effort

Building a great dental practice is a team effort. Dentists, no one expects you to do it all by yourself.

As you create an amazing team, focus on including your team members as your valued crewmates. I learned so much from my father about being a leader and also being a member of a great team. My dad was also a great coach. Well, not literally, but being the man of the house, he paid the bills, fixed the cars, plumbed the toilets, planned the meals, kept us as safe as he could from any major trauma, and so forth. He understood the big picture of keeping our home functioning at its highest capacity and being the leader of our house. Each year I aged, he showed me how to become a grown-up, trusted me, and gave me more and more responsibility. He put me in charge of balancing his checkbook, changing the oil in the car, fixing a flat tire, cooking one day a week for the family, and yes, unclogging toilets. Imagine if I moved out as an adult and he did everything for me my whole childhood. How well would I do in the real world? At first, I used to think I was free labor, but later, I realized he empowered me to be independent and successful.

Wouldn't it be great if your shipmates were more independent? When the whole team understands your vision and works together to get to their dream destination, success can be achieved for everyone. In the tips I will share in this book, every team member should benefit.

Give a man a fish and you feed him for a day.
Teach a man to fish and you feed him for a lifetime.
—Lao Tzu

Let's Have Some Fun! Count the Tips

When I wrote this book, I intentionally added thousands of dollars' worth of tips! I challenge you to find these hidden treasures. As you read these upcoming chapters, I encourage you to count the tips and calculate how much it could improve what you bring to your practice. #Priceless

Time to Cast Off from the Dock

Let's take the leap of faith and step into the unknown. By leaving your comfort zone, your current routine, and trusting the perfect coach for you, you'll have an experience that you will cherish forever or, depending on which coach you choose, get results that far exceed your expectations.

You will never know what's outside if you are always stuck in the belly of the whale.

Possibly, you no longer want to be an associate dentist working for someone else. You may feel like a sailor on someone else's ship when you really want to be the captain!

Read Like a Boss with Ownership Mentality

Here's your call to action: by reading this book and taking the assessments, you will begin to get my expert eyes on your practice. Treat this like using a high-tech dental cone beam on one of your patients and let's diagnose your practice! Let me help you and your teammates gain the propulsion to face the waves and go right over them. So, what are you waiting for? Your hidden treasure awaits. Let's dive in!

To all the ships at sea, and all the ports of call.
To my family and to all friends and strangers.
This is a message, and a prayer.
—Nicholas Sparks

HOLES IN YOUR BOAT

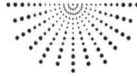

Dr. Almost Bankruptcy

Imagine that you receive a phone call on a Friday night that sounds like this:

"Heidi, I need your help. I don't know who to turn to. I am so embarrassed... I can't believe it's come down to this. I don't even know where to start, but we need to either turn in my keys to the landlord or I need to move my entire practice by Sunday night.

"I can't afford to be there one more day. The landlord posted an eviction notice for falling behind on my rent and there is no way to pay my bills, let alone meet payroll. Heidi, please help me on how to move the practice! Just tell me what to do and I will do it."

By the tone of his voice, I could tell he was in a panic and very desperate.

I thought for a moment and said, *"Wait a minute...let's think about this...moving your practice takes specialists and costs thousands of dollars to move the dental equipment. Tell me what we are talking about...how much money would it take to save your practice?"*

He was freaking out and said, *"Heidi, my rent went from $4000 a month to $8000 a month and this landlord can get away with it because the practice is in a prime location. What about my staff who* *have been with me for over fifteen years...they need their jobs. I don't want to lay anyone off, they are like family. Please, help all of us! What do I do?"*

First, I am thinking, *Only in San Francisco could you get away with raising the rent like that...*

However, having high overhead is a common problem in a dental office and my gut says, *you only need $4000, that's doable! We've got this.*

I calmed him down and said, *"Okay, listen, do you have about an hour of time for us to take a look at Monday's schedule? Because I have never seen a practice where I couldn't find some hidden revenue in their schedule. Would you be open to a quick review before you turn in your keys?"*

He emphatically said, *"Totally!! I'll make time right now or whenever you're free. Heidi...seriously, can we really do something in an hour?"*

I said, *"You bet, let's get a fresh pair of eyes on your schedule and take a look at what you have going on!"*

And as soon as I saw his schedule, about 150 ideas came to mind.

After working in dental offices for over two decades and coaching so many dentists, it gave me the experience of noticing the missed opportunities, and I saw money flying out that practice's back door. After an hour of looking at their practice's next days' schedule, I worked with him to outline all of his next steps.

Monday night, I received another phone call. Yep...this time from the office manager. He called me and was so ecstatic to say that their office had made $4600 more that day and they had scheduled $5800 more of accepted treatments. To this day, they thank me for saving their practice and they are living their dreams.

Now, they work on their social media presence, adding associates to the practice, structure rewards for the employees, fine-tune their work-life balance, and prepare for retirement. It is an ongoing journey to create a legacy for them and their children.

Can you relate to any of Dr. Almost Bankruptcy's story, or do you feel like your practice could be heading this way? Please do not be embarrassed! It's important to take action before it's too late. My client thought it was too late and that they failed; however, by working together, we steered their boat in the right direction.

Have confidence in me and let me get my eyes on your practice before you throw in the towel, because as of today, I have not had to tell someone, *"Give up or quit while you're ahead."* Have faith, stay strong, and together we can conquer some waves.

Dr. Maybe Procrastinator

Dr. Maybe Procrastinator also contacted me in a panic. He was opening their new office in a month, and all they had was dental equipment, a computer, and a building. They had no patients, no employees, big bills, and only enough money to last two months with no income. There was a lot to accomplish in only thirty days so he could become the successful entrepreneur he dreamed of being.

After creating his brand and what he would truly be known for—doing attractive marketing, hiring the RIGHT team, and training on impactful communication skills that helped their patients say, "yes," to treatment—the end result was that he grew every month. He made more than enough to take home a good chunk of change and pay his bills.

Now, we work on more systems that streamline his practice. They continue to practice how to properly reactivate patients, track specialist referrals, do amazing patient hand-offs, queuing up the doctor during an exam, keeping accounts under forty-five days old, run effective meetings, do fun team building activities, and so much more.

**Faith is taking the first step,
even when you can't see the whole staircase.
—Martin Luther King Jr.**

Changing Direction

If there are so many benefits to making a change, why doesn't everyone take the leap of faith like Dr. Maybe Procrastinator? It is because change can be scary and many of us wait until things are on fire before we grab the extinguisher. As we discussed in the first chapter, fear and resistance are common reactions. And as humans, we tend to cling to the same comfortable and familiar mindsets. These acceptable behaviors may not bring you a positive outcome, and only calculated change can navigate you from your current situation to your dreams.

As I shared in my stories, I love helping my clients see a greater picture that they may not envision for themselves. When you are working daily in your business, it can be hard to take time out of your busy life to evaluate some analytics, diagnose what you're seeing, and figure out how to develop systems that could buy back your time. Also, your perspective is limited to you, your team, and other dentists with whom you may talk.

Another issue is that what you see on social media is not always true, and tips you see on dental platforms are not always good solid sound business advice. So, in other words, you may be seeing someone who appears successful and happy, however, it could just be a façade, or you may be tempted to follow bad advice for your particular situation.

Part of protecting our positive mindset is to stop comparing ourselves to others or listening to any negativity. Don't allow others to be energy suckers! In addition, some of you may have comparanoia syndrome. This is when you see someone else, compare yourself to them, and feel you "aren't enough." The saying goes, *"It's hard to see the label from inside the bottle,"* meaning it's hard to objectively identify the holes in your boat when you are inside the hull scooping out water. And you can't see what's going on inside someone else's boat, so all you see is their shiny boat and not their issues.

I am here to tell you that you are enough and never listen to anyone who says you aren't.

Networking and referral expert Bob Burg famously said, *"All things being equal, people do business with and refer business to people they know, like, and trust."* So, when you work with someone you know, like, and trust, taking those first few steps becomes much easier.

Anything Worth Doing Is Worth Doing Well

Many times, dentists will reach out to me and ask, *"How much do you charge for your coaching?"* And deep down, I want to ask, *"How much would you charge to fix my mouth and give me a beautiful smile?"* As you can see, we need to meet, have me evaluate your practice and diagnose what you need so I can reverse engineer your goals. Plus, review options and figure out the results you want to achieve before we can see if we are a good fit. I do this because as a coach, I only succeed when my clients succeed. Frankly, I would like to maintain a good reputation. (Chuckle)

> **You can't build a reputation**
> **on what you are going to do.**
> **—Henry Ford**

I work with people whose lives I can impact and who have goals that I can help them achieve. My clients are decision-makers and action takers. Are you? Since my clients invest their money and time into making a difference, I do the time-saving work of identifying the best steps for them to take and provide the valuable resources to see projects to completion.

Plugging the Leaks in Your Practice is Priority Number 1

As the captain of your dental team, there is probably a lot weighing on your shoulders. You are technically steering the ship! You are responsible for making sure you are:

- *Hiring the RIGHT team.*
- *Leading and motivating your team.*
- *Training your employees and holding them accountable.*
- *Ensuring your team feels appreciated, supported, and trusted.*
- *Creating and maintaining a positive culture.*
- *Paying the bills while making profit.*
- *"Keeping your houseboat in order" (making sure your significant other and children are happy).*
- *Exercising, sleeping, and making time for doing the things you love.*

You are also responsible for getting the crew on your ship to:

- *Respect and appreciate you.*
- *Fill your schedule productively yet in a stress-free way.*
- *Inspire your patients to say, "yes" to treatment.*
- *Help your patients become raving fans.*
- *Not "fire" you or drown your business.*
- *Stay long-term.*
- *Keep a positive culture and meet the teams' expectations.*

While I know most people want to succeed in all of their responsibilities, many of you are not where you want to be. Some days, you might feel like you are floating along on a raft just fine when you would rather be served a tropical drink on a yacht; others of you might feel like you are barely keeping your head above water! This is when many of my clients decided to call out for my support and require me to throw them a help line. It's important to recognize the symptoms early on.

Man cannot discover new oceans unless
he has the courage to lose sight of the shore.
—Andre Gide

Let's assess your current situation. Do you...

- *Just want something more?*
- *Notice you are not growing and have plateaued?*
- *Experience frequent employee turnover or have untrained employees?*
- *Have roller-coaster income?*
- *Work more than you like?*
- *Not have as much fun as you would like to?*
- *Have issues with patients who won't "afford treatment"?*
- *Feel unable to retire or make enough profit for the lifestyle you want?*
- *Want to spoil your team but don't know how?*

Jot down a few notes here about your current practice. Remember to give candid answers. The more honest you are in your assessment, the more you can address and achieve. I am driving you to take action. If you need to spend a month doing these steps, I promise you that you will be glad you did it down the road.

Let's have you evaluate your own practice...

Are you frustrated with your dental practice, and do you have no idea what to do next or how to fix it?

Yes   No

Are you tired of being disappointed by the people you hire?

Yes   No

Do you find that your negative self-talk becomes reality?

Yes   No

Have you considered hiring a coach to improve your business but talked yourself out of it?

Yes   No

Does your schedule have open time in it and it's still not reaching your daily goals?

Yes   No

Do you have accounts that are past due?

Yes   No

Is your overhead out of whack?

Yes   No

After you or an employee discuss treatment, is the first question out of the patient's mouth *"How much does this cost?"* or *"Does my insurance cover it?"*

Yes   No

Do you lose sleep or worry about not having enough for retirement or for your family?

Yes   No

Do you want to spoil your team members but don't have the ability to do it?

Yes   No

Do you want to make a big splash in the world but aren't sure how to contribute?

Yes   No

If you answered *"yes"* to any of these questions, you've got holes in your boat! Until you plug the leaks in your practice, your money and efforts are drifting out to sea.

What are some holes in your proverbial boat?

- *Literally, holes or openings in your schedule.*
- *One-time patients who don't return (heck, some of your regular patients aren't being seen as often as they should).*
- *Patients walking out the door without paying.*
- *Unsatisfied employees.*
- *High overhead or increasing debt.*
- *Not enough in assets or retirement.*

What is the impact of these holes?

- *Spending all your time working.*
- *Feeling stressed and burnt out.*
- *Unhappy spouse and/or family.*
- *High list of unscheduled treatment.*
- *No work-life balance.*
- *Unhappy team and staff turnover.*

Obviously, this situation is NOT smooth sailing. You may say to yourself, *"Heidi, there will always be waves and a sailor must adjust."* Yes, there will always be some waves. It is normal to run into obstacles while running your practice. However, if you are seasick—losing sleep, always anxious, developing health issues, and feeling frustrated or hopeless for weeks and months—that's a sign that you need to adjust your course.

Are you sick and tired of being sick and tired? Ask yourself, *"How much is running my practice this way costing me in profit, in stress, loss of sleep, unfulfilled relationships, staff turnover, and even more?"*

Just as I felt lost and fearful when I was about to embark on the black water dive, you too may be longing for answers and find yourself looking in the dark and feeling alone.

**The pen that writes your life story
must be held in your own hand.
—Irene C. Kassorla**

Find Your Hidden Treasures

Dentists, how many of you reading this book want to make $500 more a day on tomorrow's schedule? Guess what, I mean EACH EMPLOYEE can help make this much more EVERY DAY. Employees, how many of you want to make more without working any harder? Yes, if the doctor makes more profit, there are so many ways they can reward you for your help!

By choosing to read this book, I feel like you are making a decision that you will commit to take action and believe that your life will improve from this point forward.

I am going to share how you can easily reach your goals:

- *Without buying more equipment.*
- *Without adding more employees.*
- *Without taking another continuing education course.*
- *Without increasing your collections by at least $500 a day and accomplishing it in a way that you will love doing.*

I will teach you how to find the hidden treasures specifically in your practice whether you are new to dentistry or have owned your practice for years. All practices have room for growth, and there are always other treasures available to you.

**A ship in harbor is safe
—but that is not what ships are built for.
—John A. Shedd**

Dr. Scratch Startup

When I received a call from Dr. Scratch Startup, he shared how they found a perfect location for a dental office, which was beautiful and plush. They had all of their equipment, their website, everything they needed, except for one thing.

The dentist called me and said, *"I don't have any patients! What do I do? I need employees, where do I find them? How do I bill insurance? How do we do a patient handoff or get my team trained?"*

While they were brilliant at dentistry, like many of my clients, they were not taught how to fully run a well-functioning dental business.

When I met with the dentist and his wife and listened to their vision of their ultimate business and life, I knew the steps they needed to take next and exactly what they needed me to do to coach them. Together, we branded their business to fit their life goals. We figured out how many hours they and their team needed to work, and how to attract amazing people that would be their ideal patients for the practice. We designed a plan for their new team, including whether to hire someone with lots of experience or train from scratch, creating their training materials, identifying the services they would be providing, crafting a patient avatar to use for marketing, and preparing them to open their doors.

Together, we attracted and converted 1200 people to their dental family so their gorgeous new practice had the patients they actually wanted and helped reach their goals.

When you go on a trip, you have a starting point and a destination. Before you can cast off to sea to your destination, we need to identify where you currently are and the anchors that are weighing you down.

In this chapter, you identified the holes in your boat. In the upcoming chapters, I will share the ways to not just plug the holes in your boat but also chart your course to set sail. It starts with identifying your ports of call.

On ships, a port of call is a place to load or unload cargo, obtain supplies, or undergo repairs. In the upcoming chapters, we will identify your ports of call—your processes, equipment, and resources—which will get you closer to your dream destination!

This is your call to sea! I challenge you to become the hero of your own story. How amazing will it feel when you can take the stress off your employees, find hidden treasure in your business, and create the good life you and they have always wanted? Let's start with your first port of call!

EXHAUSTED OR ENERGIZED? A STRATEGY TO WORK SMARTER, NOT HARDER

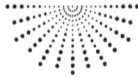

Exhausted

I want to tell you about my dad. He was a maintenance man at a large car manufacturing plant in California. He worked six days a week, fifty-one weeks a year for his entire career to provide for his family. After showing up for work at 4:30 in the morning, he'd put on his walkie-talkie and fix problems all day long.

His boss would radio him: *"Fritz, I need you to fix the robot in the paint department right away, we need to keep production going or we won't reach our goal!"*

Another man would then walk up to him and say: *"Fritz, my shoulder hurts from the repetitive motion of installing the muffler bearings overhead and I need you to find a different task for me to do."* By the way, he had to point out that there is no such thing as a muffler bearing! #Eyeroll #ReallyIThoughtTheyWereTrained

Then his radio would go off again: *"Fritz, Chris just got electrocuted and I need you to get a medic here right away!"* Yes, this guy held two big hot wires and he was the ground. Someone had to charge and tackle him like a running linebacker to get him released...they now call him "Crisp"!

Every second of every workday counts in the car industry, and when my dad got home…he was EXHAUSTED!

How many of you are completely exhausted by the practice of dentistry?

Have you ever had a time that you felt like you have tried every option available to improve your practice? Maybe you were like my dad and felt there were no options left. Then, one day someone crosses your path and says, *"Hang on, there is another option."*

I work with many offices that really need help. The truth is, they don't need to work harder or longer. Each person just needs to focus and effectively communicate about their tasks, starting with the highest priority ones.

Many times, we look at things and think, *"Can this really work for me?"*

"How can I add one more thing to my plate?"

"Am I really capable of doing that?"

Finding the hidden revenue is easier than you think, and each one of you are capable of making your business more profitable.

> **Ability is what you're capable of doing.**
> **Motivation determines what you do.**
> **Attitude determines how well you do it.**
> **—Lou Holtz**

Temptations

It can be tempting to try to save money by taking the cheapest way out there. Wasting money and time to work with a consultant who didn't help you with what you actually needed or wanted is a common mistake that we see. I don't know about you, but I can't afford to be cheap!

It's also tempting to believe that you need more new patients when you actually have plenty to accomplish your collection goals. A smarter strategy is to get patients to like, trust, and buy from you the first time you talk to them.

My advice would be to stop trying to grow your unscheduled treatment list as if you're gaining equity in your practice. Instead, learn how to properly communicate with patients and the team so treatment gets completed.

Trust me, when a dentist hires me and gets my eyes on their practice, I see the growing unscheduled treatment list all the time. It truly makes me sad, especially when the dentist had no idea the current condition of their dental practice. However, I get so excited when I can WOW a dentist and show the entire team their missing revenue, help them analyze their software and reports, plug their profit leaks, and show them exactly where to start. This shows them how to get results on the next day's schedule.

Energized

What really works to become energized is to make better and smarter actions. As a coach, I help you distinguish between what you "coulda, shoulda, and oughta" do. When I work with clients, my goal is to empower them to operate from the "present," right where they currently are, and plan for their future. In other words, together, we develop better answers and solve the issues that hold them back from a balanced life. Remember, you are adopting a growth mindset. This will positively impact your practice and the lives of others.

Are you ready to raise the bar, level up your business, and enhance your confidence? Let's do this!

First, I encourage you to set the goals you really want. No, seriously, I want you to think about something bigger than you think you can accomplish. #BigAudaciousGoals

> **Don't downgrade your dream just to fit your reality.**
> **Upgrade your conviction to match your destiny.**
> **—Stuart Scott**

Here is a portion of my goals that I put on a vision board:

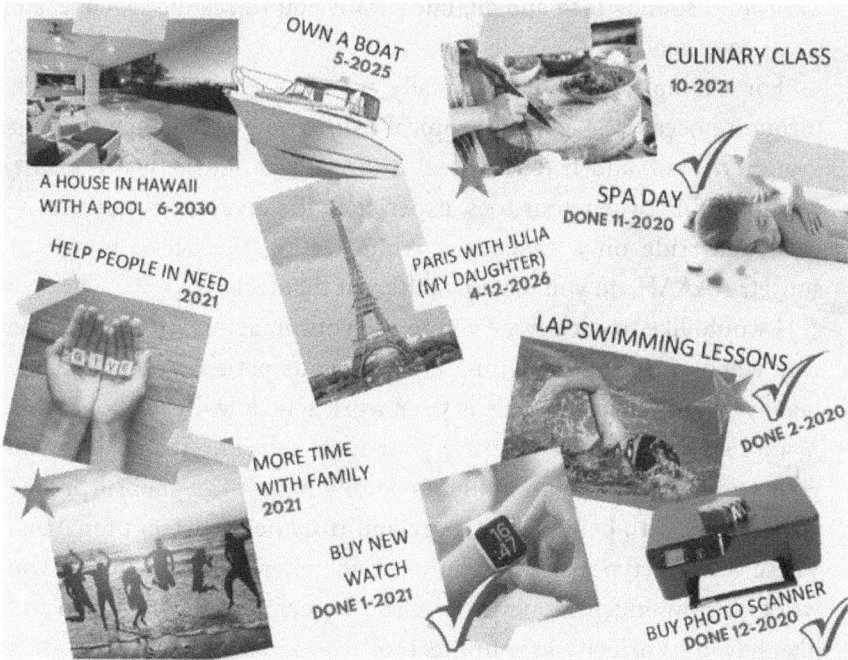

Some of you haven't even thought about important basic questions that you should answer BEFORE you set your goals. Write these in your journal. Let's do this...

- *What are the exact days and times you WANT to work?*

- *What kind of house, car, vacation, or nest egg do you really want?*

- *What tasks would you rather hire out or have done for you?*

Lots of people ask me, *"How in the world did you accomplish so much?"* Well, let's dig deeper when setting goals. *"I want to visit the Caribbean"* sounds nice and all, but I want you to really see, taste, and smell your goal.

For example, what if you really want to experience the warm turquoise ocean, the colorful tropical fish, sip on a pineapple coconut island cocktail, and listen to steel drum reggae music, feel the soft, warm sand between your toes, experience the diversity, sport beachwear, and ride on a catamaran while feeling the ocean breeze at sunset? AAAAH, do you see how different that feels?

I would like to encourage you to use your imagination in this same way when you are envisioning creating your patient schedule. Ultimately your patient schedule is your work schedule. Instead of saying, *"I want a better schedule,"* picture your ideal schedule that makes you, your team, your patients, and your family happy. Imagine surprising your family with being home more and truly being present for them. These are the types of things they remember, not how much you work or how much money you make. Remember, they want to feel like they are a priority in your life, too.

**If you think you can do a thing
or think you can't do a thing,
you're right!
—Henry Ford**

Now, let's look at your office schedule and assess how it currently runs your life. Log into your practice office software and take a look at your schedule from last week. Does it look full? Was it insane? Did everyone get home on time? Did you have open or wasted time in the schedule? Did you have patients waiting for more than five minutes? Did everyone get to eat? Did all the chart notes get entered and the billing get done? What went well or what didn't go so well? What will you do about it to improve your office and your personal life? Maybe you aren't sure how to improve your schedule, so let's take a look at this together.

It's More Than Just "Filling the Schedule"

If you are a dentist or office manager, how many times have you literally shown your team exactly what to do, where to look, and taught your employees how to help reach your production goals?

By the way, just saying, *"Hurry and fill the schedule"* does not count! It is best if you physically show your team what a perfect day looks like, how to reach the production goal, how long to schedule appointments, and what type of schedule makes everyone happy.

The truth is, even if you have a full schedule, you may not be making the money you want to make or reaching the goals that you envisioned.

Here are several action steps and systems that will add a lot of value to the practice every day and could easily energize your practice and gain more time to get more done:

- *Daily huddles.*
- *Chart review in advance.*
- *Asking for referrals.*
- *Gaining online reviews.*
- *Showing before and after photos.*
- *Reactivation calls.*
- *Roleplay all the areas that the team communicates with patients.*
- *Treatment case reviews with your team.*
- *Sending out statements with pre-programmed messages.*
- *Being chartless and paperless.*
- *Setting up online forms to fill out.*
- *Preparing in advance for what you need to accomplish the next day.*
- *Getting insurance benefits prior to the patient's appointment.*
- *Allowing patients to schedule an appointment online.*
- *Working on your marketing plan.*
- *Doing lives on social media and producing videos to share.*

Communication Key

If you recall from Chapter 2, I shared the story of Dr. Almost Bankruptcy, who was drowning in debt. He told me that he needed to move his practice within seventy-two hours. I gave them a few suggestions, and the next day they reported that they had made $4600 more and scheduled even more.

Do you want to know what we did during that hour of looking at their next days' schedule?

He logged into his practice software and got my eyes on his practice. I started off with a thorough chart review. The dentist and I looked at each and every patient coming in, reviewed their health histories, their x-rays, the intraoral photos, the unscheduled or pending treatment, and discussed how the computer was programmed.

After reviewing the patients on the upcoming schedule, we next evaluated what the dentist and the team were verbally saying to their patients. While the dentist had shared that his employees are friendly and have good customer service, I asked if he had any specific guidance for how each member of the team communicated with the patients and each other. How did they greet and seat their patients? How did the hygienist queue up the doctor prior to doing the exam? How did the clinical team communicate in front of the patient when handing them off to a front desk team member? How did the front desk present treatment and finances?

In other words, I wanted to uncover how the left hand talked to the right hand. What conversations did they have? What did they document into the patients' records? How was case acceptance tracked and reported? How do I think the patients felt with the verbiage the team was using?

The dentist took lots of notes based on what I discovered regarding Monday's schedule and what he could monitor in the future. On Monday morning, he discussed my recommendations during a morning huddle. Each member of the team was involved and everyone participated in the discussion. The dentist and the office manager explained to the team what I had suggested, and each team member followed the plan.

What I find is that most of the dental clinical team do exactly what they physically see on the schedule. If they see a crown or a prophy under their patient's name, that is exactly what they set up and do. This means, by not doing a good chart review in advance, they are completely missing the boat.

Let's Level Up Your Business

Prior to reaching out for help, this office was at a loss. The dentist, office manager, and the entire team were so overwhelmed they couldn't see where to begin. The entire team was frustrated and working to the max and some were feeling like failures. They felt they had no time to add any more to their plate. Ultimately, they were feeling stuck.

The biggest suggestion that I would like to give is for you and your team to do your chart reviews. I teach my clients to review charts two business days prior to the patient's appointment. This is where the majority of missed opportunities to grow your practice come from. Therefore, I wanted to spotlight chart review; this is the one task that employees tend to drop the ball on the most or have never learned how to properly analyze patients, and this has the biggest negative effect on your business. When my eyes are on a practice where I can evaluate your schedule in your software and SHOW you what could improve your business, 99% of dental offices boost their production per patient visit by simply doing a chart review ahead of time and following the checklist I provide.

In case you haven't heard of what a "chart review" is, I will explain. Let's think of a chart review as a thorough audit of each person scheduled. It is when you look ahead at the people scheduled and analyze every person's chart that is coming in. Every time you have an interaction with a patient, you are to make sure the person's file (name, address, email, insurance, health history, etc.) is accurate. In a chart review, we are looking at how we can make the most out of every appointment and to impress each person with an ultimate patient experience.

For example, what happens if the patient shows up for their appointment and their lab case wasn't ready to be delivered, isn't the correct case, or isn't even here in the office? Now you need to send the patient home, reschedule them, waste your setup and cleanup time when you could have treated another patient, all because someone didn't evaluate the lab case in advance.

Or, what if the patient shows up for treatment and a medical release is required from another physician before we can treat the patient? And we can't reach the doctor prior to the patient's appointment? In any event, there is no production to post and once again, you have wasted time in your schedule. In addition, that will definitely not earn us any referrals or reviews if we inconvenienced the patient, right? It is also lost production as we may have an opening in the schedule now, or it takes another opening from your future open time in the schedule when the issue could have been avoided. Didn't it take twice as much time to accomplish this appointment, too?

All of this is preventable! We must have checklists for each employee to follow to provide complete patient care AND verify they are being used. If you want the patient to feel unique and believe we care about them, we must know more than just the treatment you see on the schedule. Someone on your team should know if your patient recently had a life-changing event, a milestone to celebrate, or something personal to follow up on. For example, if you knew more, you could ask, *"How is your baby?"*, *"How are you feeling after your hip surgery?"*, or *"How did it go seeing the oral surgeon?"* Be sure we have this information documented and remind the entire team about the status of the events going on in your patient's life.

Furthermore, we need to know who has a medical issue or who is taking medications. It is amazing how many employees do not read or discuss their medical issues with the patient or the team. After all, their mouth is connected to their body, right? This should be tied into conversations with your patients when you are discussing treatment and emphasizing the importance of keeping their dental appointments. For example, you can say, *"Mrs. Smith, we are really concerned because you have diabetes..."* Plus, we don't want to reschedule just because someone didn't get medical clearance or call in a necessary antibiotic premedication needed to proceed with treatment.

Most chaos in a practice comes from not PREPARING in advance.

Upsetting your patients, the employees, and doctor(s) can be prevented by looking ahead and working as a team. Here are some things you can review on each and every patient coming in which can result in more revenue:

- *Is there still unscheduled treatment needed?*
- *Is the treatment plan accurate?*
- *Is everyone in the household scheduled?*
- *Is there a signed financial arrangement?*
- *Are the insurance benefits accurate?*
- *What are the remaining insurance benefits available to use?*
- *Do we need a pre- or post-operative x-ray or photo today?*
- *Is the appointment scheduled with the proper amount of time for each team member?*
- *Do you have family members riding to their appointments together?*
- *Are you checking to see if family members are being seen the same day who have different last names?*
- *Who can we ask for a testimonial or referral?*
- *Do we have the proper information from any specialists or medical doctors?*
- *What does each patient want for their long-term goals for their mouth?*
- *Do we have a secondary phone number and an emergency contact person on file?*

Without a thorough chart review, you may end up needing to reschedule patients, create frantic *"stop what you're doing"* and on-the-spot crisis tasks during the scheduled appointment, possibly upsetting you and your patients, and have money being left on the table, hence losing even more revenue, trust, and heart muscle.

Those of you who know me know that I want you to succeed, and I give amazing pearls from the bottom of my heart. If you haven't connected with me yet or just want to grab 10 Secrets to Increasing Revenue on Tomorrow's Schedule, go to CoachingDentist.com.

In Dr. Almost Bankruptcy's office, doing a thorough chart review created more time, more profit, more employee engagement, and helped each team member to thoroughly do their job. They were taught how to review patients in advance, which also minimized chaos and open time in the schedule. #JobSatisfaction

I believe that every practice should be able to make more if they focus on a few key metrics that would make the biggest difference for their office and in the shortest amount of time. By focusing on improving a couple of these systems listed, you can easily make $500 more on tomorrow's schedule.

What is a key metric, you ask? Well, a key metric is something we can track, measure, evaluate and improve. When I am coaching my clients, I custom design specific key metrics that will help each team member on where to focus, strive to improve, report, earn a bonus, and we all celebrate their wins. When I suggest my custom-designed key metrics and help the dentist set forth goals, it must be a win-win-win. This means what we do is good for the patient, you, and the employee.

I would like to recommend that you track and report your numbers. You should all know the saying by now, "What we track we can improve." There are many things we can analyze in advance, discuss at the huddle, take action on, plug gaps on, and prevent money from walking out that door every day. It is up to you to commit to locking in better habits, having a positive outlook, and improving your annual numbers that lead to profit.

Heidi's Promise:

If you become a client after reading this book, I will give you a comprehensive analysis on your practice and show you how to work less and be more profitable every day.

Speaking of employees, did you provide them with this book? Your employees are smart and want to learn more. Let them read my book, get inspired, use their creativity and then schedule a thirty-minute team meeting to discuss their ah-ha moments, ideas, or listen to what they feel the team needs to improve.

Be encouraged by their initiative and appreciate the pearls each person discovered and let them exchange thoughts about what resonated with them. Talk about what is going well with some of these systems that I have listed. Then, say, *"Okay. team, tell us what we can do to improve this dental practice."* Make a list, create some action items, and have each person commit to creating better habits. Then, schedule another meeting to discuss your wins and celebrate their efforts.

Let me give some example key metrics that you could use to set goals with your team and level up your practice:

- *Patients are seated within five minutes of their appointment time.*
- *Account receivables are within normal limits when looking at the 30-, 60-, and 90+ day buckets.*
- *Treatment case acceptance excluding what insurance pays for is over 40%.*
- *No-shows or short notice cancellations are under 5% per provider.*
- *Adults being seen in hygiene have a 3:1 ratio for periodontal codes versus preventative prophylaxis codes being posted.*
- *Payroll is under 23% of total collections (this includes all costs to employ that team member).*
- *Insurance is paid within forty-five days on the "bread and butter" dentistry.*
- *Assure prospective patients that call the office get converted into the schedule and show up for their appointment with their new patient forms done in advance.*

- *Set a goal to have one hundred more reviews than your local competitor.*
- *Expect that employees ask daily for reviews.*
- *Aim for a 90% pre-appointment rate in the hygiene department.*
- *Check to make sure daily production and collection goals are met.*
- *Make sure new patients get scheduled within a week.*
- *Keep your supply bill under 7% of yearly average collections.*

My hope is that by writing this book, it will show you and your team where to focus, relieve weight off your shoulders, encourage open communication, empower growth, increase positive acknowledgments, and offer you high-level information.

Sometimes, the team needs to understand why we behave the way we do. We are all unique, with different personalities, and I would love to explain what each personality's strengths and non-strengths are. Part of adopting a growth mindset includes enabling your team to be more understanding towards each other and hopefully, you will learn how you can better support each other.

Did you know that I do a-la-carte services? Yep! Just email me at Heidi@CoachingDentist.com, and ask to reserve a fun team meeting with me. Together, we can address these underlying issues with a team bonding experience.

4

CHALLENGES:
DOUBLE YOUR LEVEL OF
WILLINGNESS

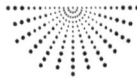

Back to the Future

Some of you may not know that I have been in dentistry since 1989. Boy, has the industry changed a lot! I doubt any of you today would work in an office similar to the first one I worked in…but I was committed to helping patients get healthy.

Back in the '80s, it was all the rage to have a "front deskless" office.

Our patient flow looked like this: patients were told to wave to the team as they peered through a saltwater fish tank. Once the insurance coordinator saw them waving through the tank, they pressed a button to alert me that my patient arrived.

When I saw the light, that indicated that my patient had arrived. I went out to cheerfully greet them and walk them to their operatory. There, I showed them where to put their belongings and their seat, reviewed their medical history, explained what we would be doing that day, and let the dentist know we were ready.

After I assisted, the dentist left, and I gave the patient post-op instructions, collected their money, and scheduled their next appointment. After I walked them to the door and said, *"goodbye"* and *"I look forward to seeing you next time!"*, I quickly went back to sanitize the room, sterilize the instruments, order and stock supplies, made post-operative calls, and reactivated patients, reported to the doctor, and then treated the next patient. (I had to use my time very efficiently to complete all of these tasks, as the patients and my team counted on me to get it done.)

Don't even get me started on the paper book scheduling and the erasing we did all day long in the '80s. Using our pegboard accounting system, we were lucky if we got our insurance benefits by looking through a microfiche disc. It took five to ten minutes to scroll around to find a particular insurance company to look up the patients' dental insurance benefits. I really envy the employees today who get to work with high technology and work with dentists who invest in their team.

The only way this office could get everything done was to have all of our systems be really efficient! Later, my former bosses would reach out and say, *"I've never had an employee as efficient as you! You are rare! I need you to teach the team the way you did it. The office ran smoothly and the patients were really happy."*

What worked years ago, of course, doesn't work today. I share this to let you know from an employee's point of view that I know what works well and what doesn't. Just so you know, when I get my eyes on your practice, I bring new and fresh ideas!

And times are always changing at the speed of light. Now, we can seamlessly do so much! What is the one aspect of the business that never changes? Patient expectations.

While we can have all the technology in the world, when it comes to running a dental business, our patients consistently expect to be treated well. Let's face it: they probably don't want to be there, and they want a pleasant patient experience. Put yourself in their shoes...you are getting into their personal space...where they eat...where they kiss...and they are super nervous about what you are going to find and how much things could cost!

One thing that most offices could improve is to refine their people skills to grow the practice. We need to not treat people as if they are an interruption or just a number.

Let's think about this: when you go to a business, have your expectations always been met? Have you consistently had great service, or have you been disappointed at times? Can you actually refer that business to your friends and family not knowing what type of service they will receive when they come in?

It is incredibly important to consider every interaction with every person you come into contact with. Every time someone comes into your office or calls the office, you want them to feel like they are being treated as if they are your best friend who you are greeting at the airport.

Your patients should love coming into your office so much, they ask, _"What does it take to get a job here?"_ When you give patients something positive to talk about, they become your raving fans.

I want to share an experience I had during a medical procedure under anesthesia. I don't know about you, but I am seriously terrified to be "put under the knife." I recall being wheeled into the sterile surgery room, laying down, and one person came up to me and said, _"Hello, Heidi, my name is Sue, and I am going to take really good care of you."_ I just had a blank stare as she went to finish setting up.

The next nurse came in, walked up by my side, touched my shoulder and said, _"Hello, Heidi, my name is Bob. I am going to make sure you are very comfortable."_ I nervously said, "Great!"

Another nurse came in smiling, stuck out her hand to shake mine, and said, _"Hello, Heidi, my name is Cindy, I will be assisting the doctor, monitoring your vitals and making sure everything goes smoothly, okay?"_ I just looked up at her with the tiniest smile, thinking, _She seems like she is confident in what she is doing._

How can you give your patients an experience that they actually care to share with others? I have shared this story so many times and recommended that medical facility to so many of my friends and family members. The funny thing is that my referrals or word of mouth had NOTHING to do with the actual quality of the procedure done by the doctor. I recommended them simply because of their friendliness and professionalism. As a result, they gained so many new patients based on how well they treated me. #FreeMarketing

Here are some easy and practical things you can do to impress your patients.

You can create such a great vibe in your office that they love coming to their dental appointments. This is where everyone listens to others and talks cheerfully and respectfully. One way is to make sure of it is to cheerfully introduce yourself and others in the office to the patient and tell them how you will take care of them.

Your warm and friendly tone of voice will set you apart from your competition. When you speak with a friendly tone, along with a mindset for connection, you are more likely to be trusted. Use people's names and say edifying things to those around you. The most important word to a person is their name. Therefore, make sure you talk to your patients and co-workers using their names with a friendly tone at least three times during their visit.

Also, build rapport and find ways to create future conversations. Patients are excited when you remember things about them. Start documenting personal things in the patient note area that you can get to really quick. Many offices have these detailed conversations buried in old chart notes and we can't find them and refresh our memory fast enough. Learn their children and pets' names, hobbies, travel, anniversaries, or current life events going on with them. They love your follow-up and knowing that you listened. Of course, we can't possibly remember all this, so be sure to update your team on the documentation that you reviewed prior to the patient coming in. Notice how your patients smile and say *"Oh, I can't believe you remembered that!"* Trust me, they are impressed.

Frequently when I am contacted to do an initial practice analysis, I notice how many times important tasks are ignored and money is left on the table. For example, even when the same patient has been there five times and had at least seven touch points with different team members along the way, and I ask the team, *"Tell me what you know about this patient,"* many times, I get a blank stare and they look at each other for answers and not one person can remember or find something to tell me in a chart note showing a personal thing about that patient. How would you feel if you were the patient and someone asked about your husband and you responded with, *"I told the front desk that we are divorced and to remove him from my insurance!"* It is imperative that we take the time to listen to our patients and have a good communication system within the office to minimize embarrassment.

And believe me, patients do feel the negative or positive vibe in the office. It is very important to maintain an upbeat culture, focus on the patient's needs, and keep our personal lives to ourselves. This means that we will need to be more patient-centered and show them we truly care about them. After all, they are paying a lot to be there and deserve to have our full attention.

Another way to show the patients how great the office is would be to display a team culture coffee book. This is an interesting photo album displaying office team-building events, happy images, testimonials, or stories and letting the patients get to know you and your team.

I call these personal touches doubling your willingness to connect with your patients. All of this will help in improving our mindset and theirs! The results of this will be:

- *Gaining new patients.*
- *Having patients trust, like, and buy from you.*
- *Minimal employee turnover due to a positive environment and great leadership skills.*
- *Obtaining online testimonials.*
- *Achieving a well-known brand around the community.*

I challenge you to double your level of willingness and see what happens.

As part of your chart review, you may discover which patients have a Facebook account, Yahoo email or Gmail email address. Guess what? If they do, and they pay you a compliment, it's a perfect opportunity to ask them for an online review. One action step that you could focus on is listening for the compliments they pay you. If a patient says, *"I didn't even feel his shot!" "I love my new smile!"* or, *"You all are so nice here!"* it's the perfect opportunity to ask for a review. Please take the opportunity to ask your patients to share their great experience.

You can say, *"Thank you so much (patient name). We really appreciate your compliment, and we would love more patients just like you. You know that most people shop for a dentist by going online and reading the reviews. Would you mind if I sent you a link right now so you could share your feedback online for us?"*

How does that sound, guys? Trust me, nothing I teach will be too difficult for anyone to accomplish. I will customize my coaching to your personality.

Are you seeing the importance of a simple chart review? Did you know you will have better results—a greater ratio—from asking brand new patients for referrals than from asking your existing patients? Be sure to add that to your new patient flow checklist. Trust me, that one script can bring you more patients and more online reviews which give you more credibility. Imagine if each new patient made you $10,000 over the next ten years...all these systems I mentioned are imperative to a growing dental practice. Which one will you be working on over the next ninety days and celebrating the results it brings?

You may need to improve some mindsets in your office, role-play with each other, and get more comfortable with improving your communication skills. Some of you need to take a deep breath so you can really connect with your patients, remove sources of stress, get more support, structure your talks with patients, and redesign how you spend your time.

Many dentists hire me for a-la-carte services to help develop specific checklists, create spreadsheets, train and role-play with their team, or get creative ideas on how to solve issues going on or motivate the team. If you are interested, simply reserve a call with me on the link in my website CoachHeidiMount.com and we can see if we are a good fit to work together. I promise, no pressure here. The key is to work on something that will improve your life so you don't have the same "ole" results.

THE KAIZEN PHILOSOPHY
IMPROVES CAREER SATISFACTION

Kaizen!

My dad proudly worked for a company called New United Motors Manufacturing, a company that combined the Japanese company, Toyota, with the American company, General Motors. As a result, their company leadership style was often influenced by Japanese work culture. This included the philosophy of continuous improvement. The Japanese word to describe this "change for good" is *kaizen*.

Whenever my dad saw me doing chores and getting distracted, he would quickly say, *"Kaizen!"* This was his shorthand way of saying to me, "be focused and efficient." I am sure he realized in the past that nagging didn't work for me. Saying, *"Kaizen!"* always made me laugh and got me to complete my chores faster. He did his best to create a fun and productive environment for me.

We all want a positive outcome in our everyday life. While we may strive to be more focused and efficient, and to be able to say that we use the concept of kaizen in all areas of our life, often we aren't sure how to achieve this goal or which steps would be more efficient.

So far, I have shown you how to dream bigger, to delegate, and to identify which holes to plug. We've examined mindsets you may struggle with, potential pitfalls in your office, how profits can transform your life, which commitments to make, and action steps to take. Now, let's concentrate on the entire team's emotional needs. Yeah, I know some of you want to avoid this topic. However, understanding how the team feels and thinks is incredibly important.

We all have different titles, education, upbringings, desires, and expectations, and we are all unique individuals. Now, I would like to share with you what I have discovered over the past few decades about what each position seems to crave.

Let's break this down into specific departments. Here are good examples of what the dentist/owner wants from the employees:

- *Maintain a positive attitude and set the tone for the office.*
- *Communicate effectively with patients and the team.*
- *Take pride in their work.*
- *Do all of the tasks in their full job description without reminders.*
- *Report their actions and what they accomplished.*
- *Represent their mission and vision for the practice.*
- *Show commitment to teamwork.*
- *Demonstrate professionalism and be courteous.*
- *Adaptability and being coachable.*
- *Appreciate the job opportunity and benefits provided.*
- *Foster an "ownership" mentality.*
- *Be productive and offer others help when there is open time in the schedule.*

So, in other words, team members, as the captain of the ship, your boss wants you to show respect, be accountable for your own tasks, and bring a positive attitude at all times. It's important to understand the sacrifices they have made to own and run their dental practice. Imagine going to school for over a decade and spending hundreds of thousands of dollars for college and more when purchasing a dental practice.

Team members, I want you to think about how you would evaluate your strengths using the list below. Circle the number at which you

would rate yourself, with ten being the highest and one being the lowest. Please give this some thought, and do an honest self-assessment. If you are really bold, ask the entire team to anonymously rate you, too.

Maintain a positive attitude and set a nice tone for the office.

10 9 8 7 6 5 4 3 2 1

Communicate with patients so well that they aren't confused about their treatment, their account, or their post-operative care.

10 9 8 7 6 5 4 3 2 1

Communicate with co-workers, dentist(s), and management so well that people are not frustrated by lack of charting, unfinished tasks, or poor follow-through; you don't start or participate in any drama.

10 9 8 7 6 5 4 3 2 1

Take pride in your work.

10 9 8 7 6 5 4 3 2 1

Do all of the tasks in your full job description without reminders.

10 9 8 7 6 5 4 3 2 1

Report your actions and what you accomplished on a regular basis.

10 9 8 7 6 5 4 3 2 1

Represent the mission and vision for the practice at all times.

10 9 8 7 6 5 4 3 2 1

Show commitment to teamwork.

10 9 8 7 6 5 4 3 2 1

Demonstrate professionalism and being courteous.

10 9 8 7 6 5 4 3 2 1

Practice adaptability and being coachable.

10 9 8 7 6 5 4 3 2 1

Appreciate the job opportunity and benefits provided.

10 9 8 7 6 5 4 3 2 1

Foster an "ownership" mentality.

10 9 8 7 6 5 4 3 2 1

Stay busy when you are not with a patient and offer others your help.

10 9 8 7 6 5 4 3 2 1

Now, how did you do as a team?

In your journal, I would like you to list the areas where your team excels.

In addition, I would like you to list the areas where your team needs some improvement.

Team members, congratulations on the areas in which you do great! Seriously, take a bow! Now, I challenge you to commit to improving the other areas and encouraging those that need more help. It's amazing how much more people enjoy their jobs when they have a team committed to these traits and support each other. Once we help build the business, commit to helping the dentist(s), and show them support, they will be more apt to appreciate you and give rewards. If you need ideas on how to get everyone rowing in the same direction, don't be afraid to reach out to me on Instagram @HeidiMountDentalCoach

> **Always treat your employees exactly**
> **as you want them to treat your best customers.**
> **—Stephen R. Covey**

What I have discovered is that employees want these things from their boss:

- *To make patients happy and healthy.*
- *Recognition for a job well done and hear authentic compliments.*
- *Being a part of something big.*
- *Freedom to exercise their strengths.*
- *Being able to utilize their creativity.*
- *Meaningful communication: voice their ideas.*
- *Bonding with the entire team.*
- *Maintaining a high degree of autonomy and a safe place for making a mistake.*
- *Making a decision and sticking with it.*
- *Providing mentorship.*
- *Staying up on the latest technology.*
- *To not be micromanaged.*
- *Creating a work culture by design: have a fun place to work.*

Dentists and owners, are you noticing the bottom line is that your team, the crew of your ship, need to feel appreciation, support, and trust? Learning how to be a good leader will inspire them to want to serve the practice more. This is the key to minimize crisis hiring. Dentists, maybe you need to reach out to me for a self-assessment on you as a leader so you can evaluate yourself, too.

Many dentists have me coach them privately to help them learn how to motivate and lift their team to their highest potential. You are welcome to reserve a call with me and have a conversation about your leadership style. I am here to rescue you from pirates who steal your joy or rob your freedom.

> **Leaders must be close enough to relate to others,**
> **But far enough ahead to motivate them.**
> **—John C. Maxwell**

Let's take a moment to think about what I just taught. How many issues would be solved in your practice if each person met the needs of others instead of blaming someone else? What if we all took responsibility for ourselves? After all, when you point your finger at someone else, you have three fingers pointing back at you.

You may be asking yourself, *"So, where do I begin, Heidi?"* Well, I believe that the majority of offices have these issues because they do not have a clearly defined business plan. Most doctors have not even written down their own mission statement or vision for their life, let alone develop a list of traits for the team to abide by. This is where I help my clients achieve the highest level of growth.

We can create an environment that employees WANT to work in. Imagine if you and your team created the traits that everyone needed to follow, and if they don't, they can't work at your office. What a way to onboard a new employee, to protect everyone from drama, and minimize employee turnover! How cool would that be?

Common Myths Among Dentists and Team Members

It's tempting to say, *"Our business will grow if we just buy this new shiny object,"* or, *"What we need to do is hire more people,"* or, *"We just need more new patients!"* Actually, 95% of the time the real issues are inefficient systems, dentists throwing spaghetti at a wall trying to see what sticks, and untrained team members are doing the best with what they know.

Many colleagues ask me, *"What is a system?"* A system is an organized method in which we get something done. As a coach, I will need to help you create the most efficient way to run your practice according to the factors involved so you can reach your long-term goals. I act as a compass for my clients and map out the best way to navigate to the business they want.

Some of you have too many irons in the fire and need to slow down. When you get my eyes on your practice, I help you prioritize and relieve weight off your shoulders. What we will do is choose a couple of systems and make sure that the entire process efficiently functions. We begin by giving you simple tasks to work on, I provide the time-saving resources with checklists, and this will help you buy back your time. By providing my expertise and customized resources, I will help you and your team simplify your processes and improve how your business flows.

Let me list some examples of systems that you or your team may want to improve:

- *Your "brand" (this is way more than your website and logo!).*
- *Leadership: implementing and reinforcing policies created.*
- *Pre-clinical exams and communication skills so patients can trust the dentist more.*
- *Scheduling to goal without chaos.*
- *Minimizing no-shows and short-notice cancellations.*
- *Front desk phone skills and new patient process.*
- *Team meetings. #NotAComplaintSession*
- *Accountability without micromanaging.*
- *Managing the employees where they respect and trust you.*

- *Proper patient hand-off or "trust transfer" to avoid the hallway of amnesia.*
- *Queuing up the dentist for the exam where the patient sells themself on treatment.*
- *New and emergency patient protocols to avoid frustration in the back.*
- *Developing a standard operating manual where tasks can be handled by another person.*
- *Reactivating patients so they actually schedule.*
- *Internal and external marketing where you attract more of your favorite patients.*
- *Financial arrangements and collecting from patients to minimize past due accounts and to help patients value your services.*
- *Referrals and testimonials where patients are your raving fans.*
- *Ordering supplies to stick with the budget and minimize overstock while always having what you need.*
- *Monitoring and improving key performance indicators so each person knows how to improve their department and celebrate their wins.*
- *Appreciating your team to minimize employee turnover.*

It's important to discuss, train, and practice systems as a team. Each person needs to understand how their job affects other departments. Wouldn't it be fun to switch roles so we truly understand why following checklists are so important? I like to discuss why we do things the way we do and get everyone on the same page. Otherwise, the front office team thinks the back office should speed up while the back office is wishing they knew how to schedule correctly. We know that most of the time we would love to have other people try to do our job, however, this is nearly impossible to achieve. Therefore, employees count on strong leadership and a clear business foundation to be in place; otherwise, employees tend to leave.

It is paramount to understand that when your team is **listening** to you teach, they are **hearing** you; when your team is **talking** and physically involved, they are truly **learning.** When an owner can present why the system is so important and hold others accountable, things run more smoothly. Because if one area falls short, it will quickly affect other areas in the practice. When team members are doing things differently or if they are not updated on new office protocols, people become frustrated and feel left out. True systems that are developed and mastered always produce results!

Dentists invest into marketing to acquire patients, not to have them thrown overboard. Dentists spend money on websites, search engine optimization, professional marketers, radio ads, signage, brochures, online scheduling, phone lines, landing pages, mailers, virtual assistants, welcome or referral gifts, graphic artists, and much more. It's very rare that I meet a dentist or a team member that knows the true cost of acquiring a patient. This is something each office should know. You can easily track marketing expenses, patients who inquire about your office, how much production is produced, and how much you collected. A huge profit seepage is when you pay for all this marketing and the prospective patient is not converted into your schedule. That is a big facepalm moment! #BlewIt What I teach my clients is the importance of converting their prospective new patients into the schedule and how to accomplish it. My motto for every interaction is:

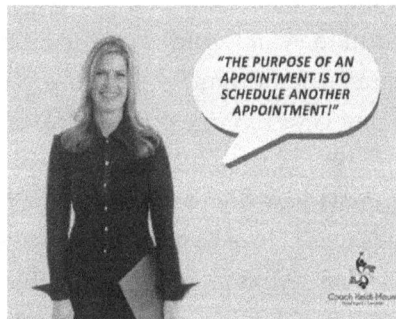

In my opinion, your new patient process is one of the most important systems to have implemented. Let's face it, dentists spend a lot of money on acquiring new patients. Studies have shown that for every four prospective shoppers who contact your office, you will probably only gain one person that schedules a dental appointment. The average dental office presents four treatment plans to get one person to schedule a dental appointment. That means it could take your office answering sixteen phone calls with prospective new patients to fill four treatment appointments for the doctor. Then, the challenge is getting the patient to value all of the treatment recommended, commit to show up for their appointment, and have the money to pay any out-of-pocket fee.

Training your employees on the communication skills for your new patient calls is imperative to grow your practice. You may need to identify who should be the first point of contact in your office. Too many times, I see the newest employee answering the phones and not offering an appointment, let alone scheduling the person who called. Let's make sure we capture revenue on the front end...when the "shoppers" call your office.

I help the employees with their phone skills, get them more comfortable, teach them to ask power questions, and gather the most important information. I recommend customized scripts and check-lists to be placed in an easily accessible standard operating procedure manual, to practice role-playing, and to record and review some conversations and master this process. Once you can track your new patient process, measure the treatment results, and improve your numbers, then you know you can run like a well-oiled machine.

The ultimate goal is to get the prospective patient to say "yes," right? Know that shoppers do not know which questions to ask when they call. They will mostly ask things like, *"Do you take my insurance?"* or *"How much is a cleaning?"* They don't ask good questions like, *"Has the dentist ever been sued for malpractice?"* So, what is a proven way to accomplish a "yes" when someone calls your office and asks a question that shouldn't determine finding the best fit for you and your family and you want to take control of the conversation...Here is what I recommend saying: *"That is a great question, sounds like you are looking for a new dentist. Am I correct?"*

Next, we spend a minute building rapport and documenting the details in your software. This is what I work on with my clients so we don't lose patients right from the get-go. Most of the time when I ask team members about the new patients, we mainly get their name, insurance, and demographics. Therefore, we don't know ANYTHING personal about the person or how to customize their dental visit.

Let me help with this and you will discover how to improve your new patient visit.

Anyone who is trained and answering the phone should find out information from our prospective patients such as:

- *"How can we make your visit more comfortable?"*
- *"What is important to you when choosing a dentist?"*

Did you notice that I recommend asking open-ended questions? This is the only way to get patients to stop, think, and tell us more useful information. So, what will this information do for us? Well, if a patient tells you, *"Just don't show me a needle!"* or *"The hygienist better not lecture me about flossing!"*, you can tailor their dental appointment in a way that won't upset them.

How about we try to add more profit during that phone call? Would you like that? Great, start asking, *"Is there anyone else in the household who we can schedule?"*

Maybe to buy back some of your time, we have the patient bring in a rundown of their dental benefits. How much time are we spending punching buttons with their insurance company? This is a time-consuming task. What if we say, *"Mrs. Mount, if you can go online and type in your subscriber identification and bring us your dental insurance details, we will be able to translate it for you and let you know if you have any out-of-pocket expense."*

I can totally hear some people right now saying, *"That won't work!"* Well, I say to you, what if it does? It has been done successfully with my clients. Try it consistently for three months on all patients who are part of the younger, more tech-savvy generation. Remember, we are in charge of our own business and how we spend our time.

Change your mindset and approach regarding your shopping patients and you will notice better results. This means we do not lie, act inconvenienced, or prejudge people. We need to give everyone the chance to be a great patient and say *"yes"* to our best care. After all, even if their insurance doesn't pay your office, your kindness will be remembered and you could gain new patients in the future.

If our goal is to give everyone something positive to talk about, then why would we not WOW every person that we come into contact with? #Reputation So, take the time to sit down and create an action plan or flow chart to help build your practice. Without an action plan or flow chart, there will be missed opportunities and lost revenue every single day you show up for work. It is important to find a way to prevent money from walking off the plank and do our best at giving our patients what they truly want.

Okay, talk to me...

1. **On a scale of 1-10, how important is your practice or your career?** _____
2. **On a scale of 1-10, how would you rate the status of you feeling truly successful?** _____

Now, in your journal, write down what is holding you back from getting from answer #2 to answer #1.

Some of you need to take the time to define what success would look like to you. For decades, I had the mindset to just make enough to pay my bills. I didn't know there were ways to live a better or more fulfilling life until I hired a coach. To this day, I always have a coach... sometimes more than one. (Probably because I need more help than most people.) My coaches see things from a different perspective, hold me accountable, and help me accomplish more.

There is usually a gap between where we are and where we want to be, right? As your coach, this is necessary for me to know. This is part of our plan to solve problems, implement a course of action, and create your new life. I want to help you stay on track with balancing your work and your personal life. It's important to do things where people will still like you, eh?

Business and personal growth will accelerate when you create enough room for it to happen.

Dentists hire a coach because they know the value of sharing ideas with someone who understands them. I like to be subjective enough to want a lot for them. When you talk to the right coach about your options and they know how to ask the RIGHT questions, the difficult and confusing issues become very clear. It is time to stop starting and stopping and develop a clear path.

Let's face it, when you have fewer problems and you get to work with your whole heart, you feel better and live happier.

6

TIME TRAVEL—
STRATEGIES TO USE TIME WISELY

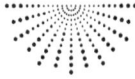

Dr. Already Successful

A very successful dentist hired me to get business coaching. While he made plenty of money and had lots of patients, he knew there was room for improvement. Requesting a clear business plan, he wanted to *"figure out how to prevent burnout of his staff."* He wanted a less chaotic schedule, more time off, and to prepare for retirement. He said, *"I want all 'these things' and I need your help to tell me how to get it!"*

We started off with long-term goals. He was about fifty years old and stated that he would like to retire in ten years. He admitted to having high blood pressure, which scared him.

His roadblocks, which made it difficult to reach his goals, included sleep deprivation, an all-consuming lifestyle, no goals, and no written plan. Lacking deadlines, he wasn't sure how to reverse engineer his goals. He trusted me and he said, *"Hold my feet to the fire and keep me accountable. Just tell me what to do next and I will do it."*

I showed him how to fully serve his patients and keep them healthy, taught what each team member could do to help reach the big picture for our patients' desires, and had him set up a tracking method of where the schedule was and where it ended up. He consistently sent me videos and reports showing me how he was making more than $5100 more a day. It is pretty exciting. He is now one happy businessman and asked me, *"Why didn't the last consultant teach me this?"* (I hear this a lot!)

Five months into coaching, he started to believe that he could retire in five years. After only nine months of coaching, I think he can taste retirement. Since he works a lot less, he and his wife have started to take romantic weekends away on private jets! He now has a taste of the good life and loves the lifestyle he created. As we set bigger goals, he just kept accomplishing more and more. Dr. Successful trusted that my action steps would land him the results he wanted. Best of all, he has a full nest egg to care for his family's future. Oh, and dentists keep reaching out to purchase his attractive practice. We keep improving his business, which makes his office more valuable. He, his wife, and I are grateful that he can retire any day he chooses.

On another exciting note, I helped him become a coach for new grads and develop another business that he can do while working only four days a month, as he considers this fun. He has a passion for mentoring younger and newer dentists and helping them prevent the pitfalls of practicing dentistry. The key is to bring out the best in you, fan that fire, and help you get to where you want to be. #LifeJourney

Do you believe in time travel? While time travel seems like an illusion, so is the thought, *I don't have enough time.* While you can't control everything, you can control what you spend your time on. So, the next time you feel like there is not enough time, I would like you to examine what you did in the past twenty-four hours. Literally, track everything you spent time doing each item. Then, evaluate which habits, distractions, tasks, and time-wasters you could eliminate.

I want you to see how you can take your team and your office from where you are to where you can be in one day! #TimeTravel Having spoken to hundreds of team members all over the world, I understand which tasks are involved for each position and how long each one should take. When we give employees things to do and they mention, *"We don't have time,"* sometimes they are correct. They are running around and very busy. Unfortunately, being busy doesn't always help a business grow. There is a difference between being busy and being productive.

Some team members are frustrated and exhausted from so much busyness. What I hear is that a lot of frustration comes from other employees who don't finish their job or when their boss keeps adding things for them to do. For example, an employee may say:

- *"I couldn't seat the patient because I had to upload the new patient forms and records from the previous office, which made me run late."*
- *"I didn't know what to schedule or quote because there were too many treatment plans and the chart notes weren't finished."*
- *"I was trying to work on past due accounts, but the doctor told me to stop and fix the schedule."*

Treat the Cause Not the Symptom

Think about if you were to see a medical doctor for a tummy ache. The doctor can fix the issue with pills. However, wouldn't it be more important to get to the root of the problem and fix the cause? So many offices want to make more profit so they jam in more patients. This only leads to upsetting people and exhaustion. It takes a "specialist" to properly diagnose your practice and prescribe the best way to prevent issues.

By following my clear and unique systems, we actually create more time. So, how do we create more time? This may sound Jedi, but we have ways to tackle your busy schedule.

Remember when I talked about doing a chart review ahead of time? Just think if you spent a few minutes on each patient coming in and PREVENTING chaos on the day of their appointment. How much smoother would your day be? What if you no longer had the chaos of rescheduling patients, trying to reach the lab, insurance companies, pharmacies, previous dentists or other medical providers during their appointment time? It's so frustrating for everyone when things should have been dealt with in advance.

If you have to send patients home, it costs you a ton. Let's say you make $100,000 a month and you work 112 hours. That means you could lose about $892 for the hour of open time in your schedule. The entire team must understand what your office needs to make per hour to run your business and what it needs to make in order to earn more income and make a profit. After all, bonuses and raises come from profit earned.

When the team does not work together to schedule, collect, or do things right the first time, it costs us more time and money in the follow-up process. None of us want to feel like we are harassing patients, finishing someone else's job, or doing extra work, right?

While the schedule dictates everything we do, it also is in charge of what can be accomplished. If the schedule isn't effective, people will be frustrated. I have never met a team that enjoys a slow or crazy schedule. They usually tell me that they want a meal break, to not go home exhausted, and to work in a thriving dental practice. That seems fair, doesn't it?

So, how can we make everyone happier? Many of us just need to manage our time wisely. Let's get you organized by taking the first part of our day to strategically plan how we will use our time. Okay, I already sense some negative thinking..."I have tried that, but the day gets crazy, Heidi!" Please trust me on this. Try this for one month, keep a record, and watch what gets done.

Write the five items that you must get done and how long it will take to get it done. Then, put it in the calendar and assign a time to get your list done. For example:

- Monday 8:00–8:15 a.m. Review chart notes and appeal Mr. Nice Patient's insurance claim.
- Monday 8:15–8:45 a.m. Reactivate 10 patients.
- Monday 11:00–11:25 a.m. Prepare for the team meeting.
- Monday 1:00–1:20 p.m. Review finance charges prior to

statements going out. Give account receivable reports to the doctor.

- Monday 2:00–2:10 p.m. Upload team photos into the website.

You may be able to delegate particular items or assign someone to cover you so you can accomplish the task uninterrupted. I can't stress this enough: when you "wing" your day and give attention to distractions, you are NOT in control of your time or managing yourself. Most importantly, be sure to celebrate your accomplishments and visualize your true north!

Rarely do we experience true emergencies that prevent us from getting our list completed. More likely, attending to diversions and lack of focus are keeping you from getting your priorities done. Let's work as a team and communicate the important things you need to get done to reach the office goals. If you are proactive with reporting your results, others are less likely to micromanage you.

Live your life by a compass,
not a clock.
—Stephen Covey

Successful People Are Purposeful

We all have the same twenty-four hours in a day to advance our overall purpose in life. Successful people know the secret of how to use their time wisely to accomplish their peak purpose. This will enable you to do two things simultaneously—to laser focus on your purpose while also spending more time on the tasks that really count.

In order to propel your business, you must identify your most productive time and schedule your day accordingly. One thing I tell my clients is to set a daily goal to reactivate patients, make care calls, and complete an important project during times you have coverage or uninterrupted time during your scheduled workday. This way, you know you have a time-frame to crank it out without any excuses or distractions.

Also, I recommend setting specific times to review and respond to work correspondence so you are not being distracted by the pop-up notifica-tions all day long. Often, these notifications are not for your highest priority tasks, but because they pop up, they grab your attention and they divert your focus from the tasks that will impact the dental practice the most. Seriously, it is okay to respond to texts and emails later and not be everything to everyone while you need to take care of your own sanity.

If you are the type of person who feels stressed or submerged in thoughts, it's important to take the time to plan and prioritize your day. Instead of feeling rushed in the morning, could you prepare the night before for tasks such as writing your prioritized to-do list, gassing up your car, getting your outfit ready, or organizing your meal prep? It is important to not go to bed with an overwhelmed brain. Some of you are skipping pleasures in life and putting yourself last. What if you wake up earlier to do activities you enjoy, such as taking a walk, reading a book, or preparing your mindset for a new day? I believe this helps us be a better boss, spouse, parent, friend, and teammate.

Are you tired of getting home late? There may be a number of things you are doing that set you up for a longer workday. Have you put systems in place to prevent irresponsible patients from hijacking your schedule, people staying late typing up their chart notes, and remaining organized throughout the day so you get out within fifteen minutes after you are done serving your patient? After all, payroll is the largest expense in a dental office, and we can prevent numbers from going out of whack by sticking to a time clock policy. Remember, you are in charge of the patients in your schedule, the treatment you do, and the systems you execute. #AvoidTimeWastersAndTime-Suckers

The common man is not concerned about the passage of time, the man of talent is driven by it.
—Arthur Schopenhauer

7

ULTIMATE TREASURE—
LIVING THE LIFE YOU WANT

You Can Achieve Anything You Want

My hard-working dad was my very best friend. I say "was" because he is no longer with us. Many dads who hear me describe my love for my father and deep down care about how their children feel have asked me, *"What made your dad your best friend?"* There are so many things that help a loved one truly connect with you, remember you, and appreciate you.

My dad was consistent with his love, encouragement, and good humor. When we were together, we would be kooky in our own way and honest about life. He always held me accountable for my own actions, pushed me out of my comfort zone to be independent, and didn't enable me. (When I was a kid, I didn't appreciate this much.) He also taught me to have a servant's attitude, showed me the value of a dollar, shared what he learned about the unique personality styles, discussed marriage topics, and showed me how to handle finances. My dad always pushed me to do my very best. The traits he taught me helped me power through life struggles, made me a strong, independent woman, and helped me remember him in all that I do.

What I remember during those teaching moments is how he believed in me, empowered me, and encouraged me to grow. And it was okay to make mistakes. When I came to him with challenges or felt discouraged, he would tell me, *"Heidi, you can achieve anything you want. You just need to put the effort out to accomplish it."* Those words have carried me through my adult life. Even though my dad worked way too much, when he was off work, he was present for me. All he asked for is to not bombard him with questions or issues for at least fifteen minutes so he could unwind from work. Then, he would invite me to run to the hardware store with him or he would smile at me and say, *"Come sit with me."* This made me feel special; such a simple, small gesture can melt a daughter's heart.

My father knew how to be very effective in his schedule to make our time fun and memorable.

I knew he had a million things to do, but I think he learned that when he spent quality time with me that he actually gained time. Some of our father-daughter time was making opportunities to see who could make each other laugh the hardest or give a special gift and make the other cry.

I am so grateful for one of the gifts I gave him. It was a journal in the book *Butterfly Kisses* by Bob Carlisle that we filled out for each other. When I followed up with him, asking him if he was done answering the questions in the book, with a pouty tone he said, *"No, it's so hard to write in it, because it keeps making me cry."*

That was truly one of my favorite gifts that I bought him. Probably because I am the one who is still enjoying and cherishing every word he wrote in it. I can revisit our journal anytime I want to review the words he wrote just for me. So many funny and meaningful memories that I still cherish and laugh about. What if we didn't take the time to give special gifts or moments to each other? It's important to live life without regrets.

Cherish Your Time Available

So, how did my dad gain time? You know how kids will pester you by asking for attention? They can be relentless, right? Maybe that was just me, as I was "the Energizer Bunny"! My dad knew that the sooner we played, talked, or laughed together, the sooner he could get back to all of the other important things he had to do. #SneakyDad

How many of you have a loved one who wishes you worked less, had fewer headaches, and who wants you to take care of your health or to spend more quality time with you? Do you have someone wishing they could gain your full, undivided attention? How many calls do you avoid with friends and family because you are "too busy"? What if you had more quality time instead of excuses? I would truly love for you to be their hero, create special memories, and spend more time with them.

You see, the average person only gets to enjoy sixteen summers after retirement and every year you work is another year subtracted from your retirement. My dad wanted to retire for many years, but he was scared and didn't know exactly how. When he finally decided to retire, he only got to enjoy one summer. So instead of being my hero now, he is my angel.

Live Life To The Fullest: Final Countdown

In Chapter 3, I described identifying your perfect workday. In living life to the fullest, you need to know what that looks like. I want to show you how I help my clients and our family to create their future.

Each year, my husband and I plan our future by creating and adding to our vision board together. By vividly describing and writing down your goals you are way more likely to achieve them. Trust me, give it a try and watch the results!

Would you like a fun team-building meeting that helps your office accomplish more? Have your team create their own vision boards and display them in the break room. You can bring magazines and they can cut out photos of exactly what they want, or go online and print photos and glue them on a piece of big white construction paper.

It's fun for the team to learn about others' desires, hobbies, and personal goals they want to reach. Some people have given up, feel hopeless, think this is as good as it gets, and forgot how to have fun.

It's time to be supportive and bring more enthusiasm to work. Let's get to know each other and dream again. Start your dream boards together and learn more about each other. For example, maybe a team member wants to learn how to paint, take karate lessons, have their first spa day ever, or even something unexpected like buying some baby chicks to raise for eggs.

These vision boards come in handy when birthdays, surprise gifts, and the holidays come around (hint, hint, Docs!). The entire team can get creative and work together to accomplish the goals set and earn prizes off their vision board. Have everyone create 30-, 60-, 90-day, and yearly goals to reach on their vision board. Then, as a team, you can discuss options on how they can achieve it.

Sometimes, we need more money to fulfill some of our wishes. Money can support the things we care about most deeply, such as family, education, healthcare, charity, and fun activities. How can we make sure that you can live life to the fullest?

What if I helped your dental practice make more than your set goal? Let's say we decide to share 20% of the profit amongst the team? Imagine if you made $100,000 extra and you could share $20,000 with your team? Do you think it's a win-win? I bet your team would have a lot more smiling happening! #Energized

How many items could be checked off their vision board wish list if they gained $300, $500, or $2000 extra? How exciting would that be that you have the vehicle to help them accomplish more! You are giving your team such a great opportunity and the sky's the limit. Each person can accomplish their dreams and goals and can have the opportunity to be a hero.

I want you to stop reading this book and spend a few minutes right now to jot down in your journal what an additional 20% gets you. Doctor, take the 20% dollar amount you hit over your goal and divide it up amongst your employees. For the employees, what would sharing that amount do for you?

Work as a team and write down what you would do with your bonus or circle the items your employees could get on their dream board. Isn't this exciting and fun to do as a team?

Base Goal $_____

20% more $_____

What would I do with a $_____ bonus?

Some of you may want to:

- *Buy a gym membership.*
- *Purchase a new car.*
- *Start a retirement account.*
- *Do more for your children or church.*
- *Buy new clothes or technology.*
- *Spend more time volunteering for a non-profit organization.*
- *Read more.*
- *Help a family member out.*

Doctors, how can you be the hero for your employees? You can simply have a team meeting and ask your team what they want. Help improve their lives and elevate the team vibe. If you need ideas, message me.

It is so important to create a vision for your life and your dental practice and have the entire team supporting your decisions. Think about when you build a house…you never build a house before you engineer the design…and we would never dig a hole or pour concrete before we draw and build the house on paper.

Okay, you may be asking, *"Heidi, how are we supposed to magically gain more profit so we have more money to spread around?"*

Well, it comes from being able to strategically and properly schedule and collect from your patients every single day. Not sporadically, consistently!

The Power of Improving Your Treatment Case Acceptance

How many of you want to hear "yes" more often from your patients and schedule patients today? It starts with inspiring your patients and letting them sell themselves on ideal treatment. The key is to improve their health, confidence, and smile in a way that is meaningful to them.

What I'm known for is helping dentists make $500 more a day on tomorrow's schedule. Let me give you one of my biggest suggestions, which is to use your intraoral camera and take professional photos of your patients.

A picture is worth a thousand words...if you are not using an intraoral and extraoral camera, you are soaking up your profit and watching it evaporate. I can already hear the excuses that some of you have going on in your head.

Here are the most common reasons that I hear about the camera:

- *We don't have one.*
- *We don't know how to use it.*
- *We can't ever find it.*
- *I use it and my patient walked out without scheduling.*
- *I don't know what to say when I am using the camera.*
- *It takes two people to capture an image.*
- *Our camera isn't user-friendly.*
- *There isn't access to the camera when I need one.*

Doctors, make it easy for your team to succeed. Make sure everyone at any time can utilize a camera during a patient appointment. Another suggestion is to help them on what to say while using the camera. The number one obstacle or fear that employees tell me is that they don't use the camera because they don't know what to say to the patients when they are taking the images.

I suggest scheduling an interactive team meeting with photos and teaching them how to communicate with your patients. This means you should schedule in some time to review case studies with your team. They need to be educated themselves as most of them have not been taught or don't know what you know. In other words, what does a tooth look like when it may need a crown? Teach the team what to look for and how to inspire your patients to do treatment before they need more.

Oh, and I can't emphasize enough that if a third grader doesn't understand what we are saying, then neither will most of your patients. We should not be saying things like abutments, abfractions, torus, mesial distal split tooth syndrome, bilateral excursion, cementum, composite, interproximal lesion, radiolucency, malocclusion, all on four, and veneer. There are not enough vomit emojis for that. Heck, half the time the employees don't know what the clinicians are talking about. Please don't speak *"Dentish,"* because it is just confusing. They will walk down the "hall of amnesia" and tell your front desk they will go home and think about it. #LeftWithoutScheduling

I promise you that if you properly review your charts, schedule and collect on the same day, organize and manage your time better, have an effective team huddle, consistently utilize your cameras, and use great communication skills that each one of you can add $500 or more production every day and buy back some of your time with the profit made. Go ahead, track it!

Start by tracking tomorrow's beginning of the day scheduled production numbers and have each employee focus on adding these tips to your patients. Then, keep tracking to see who added more profit to your practice by the end of the day. Notice how much you and your employees accomplish! I would LOVE to hear your results. I have yet to find an office that didn't improve when they were properly trained in communication skills and when they are passionate about serving their patients. The most important step to remember is to celebrate your wins together.

8

THE NEXT STEPS—
HEADING TO SEA

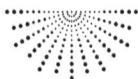

Abundance Mentality

Imagine being forced to move to another country, a place where you do not speak the language, and having to completely reinvent your life. How would you adapt? This was the reality for my family. The German invasion of Denmark during World War II caused my great-grandparents to lose their very successful commercial fishing business, and they had to start from scratch. Having eleven children, this was a huge challenge for them.

One of the eleven children was my grandfather, Aage (pronounced OH-guh). He and my grandmother, Rosa, had grown up hearing everyone discussing the big dream of being in America. On December 3, 1949, my grandparents decided enough was enough and they wanted more for their children. Migrating to America was a rough journey. They didn't speak English except the word "eggs" and had to travel on a bus with no restrooms for eleven days. My grandpa Aage's children were wrapped in wool and traveling with measles. They only remember itching like crazy and eating eggs for their meals. Then, they traveled on a cargo ship and some of the workers would put one of his children on their shoulders and sing songs to bring comfort to the children during a hard crossing over the ocean.

My grandfather, Aage, did construction in Denmark. The construction trade was different in the United States and he was so uncomfortable trying to find work in an unfamiliar country. Similarly, Rosa, my grandmother, cut hair in Denmark and had to figure out how to gain clients as a hairdresser in America. With her being shy and needing to learn English, this was quite the process.

It was extremely tough for them, especially in the early years, as they had to work hard to adjust to their new lives and country while providing for their three children. Our family had to get creative in order to thrive since they came here with nothing and knew no one. Once they connected with others, earned trust in the community, and gathered a support system life became easier.

My dad would tell me how Grandma Rosa would make homemade pumpernickel and shit on a shingle. Don't laugh, go ahead and Google that recipe. S.O.S. was an inexpensive meat, cream, and bread dish that they ate a lot. However, they could only afford meat from the same place where the ranchers bought food for their animals. Yep, they ate horse meat for a while. My grandparents traded haircuts and manual labor to put food on the table.

On a positive note, they made lots of friends who taught them the ropes for thriving in America, guided them on the steps it would take to own a home, and introduced them to Danish communities where they could connect with other Danes in the Bay Area, California. Being with the Danish people brought them so much joy and there is nothing better than a good smorgasbord. #Delish

With so many obstacles that kept arising, my grandparents could have become bitter, frustrated and/or depressed. Nothing could be further from the truth. They made sure to bring us grandkids to Danish festivals, teaching us the Danish culture and traditions. Sometimes, my family spent weeks preparing foods for the holidays and family gatherings. I always looked forward to the unique selection of food, table setting decor, and stories at my dad's family gatherings. My friends were always intrigued when I described our holidays and fun traditions. From our open-faced sandwiches, eating foods in a certain order, lightly banging our elbows on the table during a song, dancing around a Christmas tree, to being the person that found the almond in the pudding and winning a gift.

I will never forget so many decades that Grandpa Aage and Grandma Rosa provided big Danish smorgasbord meals with music, all of us singing, playing games, and with lots of laughter. I am so grateful for the love they showed us.

My grandfather was hilarious; when Grandma was in the kitchen, he would make us giggle by flicking his denture out with his tongue and it would land on the table! No matter how many times we saw him do that, it made all the kids squeal with laughter. Grandma Rosa knew what he was up to (again), and she would smile as she kindly scolded him in Danish. This silly memory really stuck with me, as I remembered vowing that I never wanted to lose my teeth, see nothing but gums, and wear a big chunk of plastic teeth!

Growing up as the first generation in such a wonderful country, my dad enrolled in the Army. Our family has a great trait of "servitude" and an abundance mentality. Even though we barely had enough for ourselves, we fed the homeless and gave what we could to others. To this day, I am very grateful for what my family taught me.

Who can you think of in your life who has influenced you? Which of their positive traits did you adopt? How could adopting their abundance mindset and characteristics positively affect your life and your practice? #TeamBuildingIdea

I recommend that you implement the steps we have discussed throughout these chapters. Many of you may feel you are already doing some of these things I have mentioned in this book. However, I encourage you to examine your practice more closely. Maybe you are not quite scheduling all of the patients you could, experiencing more employee turnover than you would like, or are not quite reaching your goals. Maybe there is something about the way your office communicates, or you need to find the proper amount of time to spend with your patients and your team. This is definitely an important area to improve if you want to reach your financial and/or emotional goals.

Sometimes, people leave the dental practice because their needs aren't being met or they think somewhere else may be better. When in fact, we just need to implement a few jaw-dropping strategies to help everyone to be happier.

Just as Dr. Ron Arndt shared the true story from Earl Nightingale in the Foreword, the poor African farmer sold his farm to seek riches in the diamond mines only to die penniless and heartbroken. Years later, the new owner of the farm discovered that the unusual rocks he casually collected from the fields of the small farm were actually worth millions—known today as the "Kimberley Diamond Mine."

Earl's moral?

Too many of us charge off on quests for greener pastures without realizing the acres of diamonds right beneath our own feet.

I share this story because many dentists have a treasure of resources and an amazing team, and yet they are not utilizing them to their fullest. When I am coaching dentists, sometimes we have to take a step backward or slow down in order to go forward faster.

Often, my clients' schedules are so crammed that they can't do what they need to do. They have too many ideas, half-done projects, unfinished business, untrained team members, and have no idea where to begin or what to focus on. This doesn't accomplish much.

Coming from a family of resilient, adaptable people and problem-solving characters, I am able to help my clients adjust their course. I am creative about solving their problems, and we work together to develop systems and habits in order to have a more productive schedule. With my eyes on their practice and their adoption of an improved mindset, they can launch faster.

When you set your mind to do something and take action, there is no reason why you can't reach your goals! We know that your schedule determines your outcome in all areas of your life. An ineffective schedule creates chaos, frustration, and unhappy people.

There must be two components to keep your schedule properly full and to reach your financial goals: patients who value your dentistry and who happily sling their credit cards at you. You see, money in a dental office is actually the result of better case acceptance and communication skills.

What are our next steps as you head to sea? We need to look outside of our patients' mouths and remember we are treating people, not teeth.

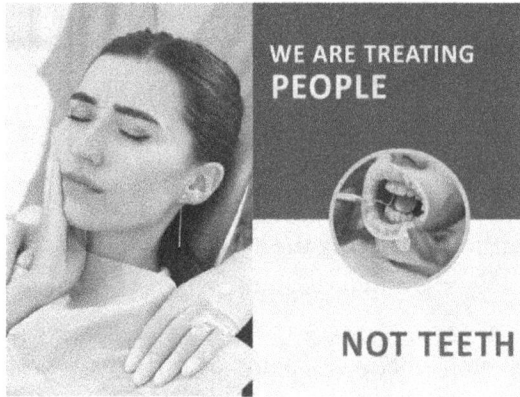

Personally, I think patients need to be a yes, yes, yes BEFORE we tell them the cost. Saying YES to treatment is recommended. So, how do we know if they are even interested in any dentistry, ready to say *"yes"* to scheduling today, or if we did a good job presenting their treatment? Well, they ask questions that show interest. In other words, we want the patient to first ask inquisitive questions. When you hear, *"How many appointments will it take?" "How soon can you get me in?"* or, *"Can you help me?"*, then you did a great job discussing how you can help your patients.

Giving Your Patients HOPE, Not Rambling Off Treatment and Fees

This means that after you presented a treatment plan to your patients, the first questions out of their mouth should not be, *"How much does this cost?"* or *"Will my insurance cover it?"* I challenge you to track and measure this process. See if you need to improve *your treatment* planning sequence or have me figure out why that is happening for you. It's best to *inspire* patients and not have the need to overcome objections. I teach my clients how to PREVENT them.

Talking About Money Can Make Anyone Squeamish

Let's talk about the uncomfortable subject...money. No one wants to discuss this, however, it's part of running a business and we must get comfortable talking about it with patients. Think about it, what happens when you go to a store to buy a gift, dress or a car. What does the sales representative ask you after they connect with you? Pretty much, *"What is your budget?"* or *"How much do you want to spend?"*

Once we know what someone can afford, they just told you the options that will not work for them. You should be able to simplify their overloaded decision-making process during the financial arrangement and show them exactly how they can afford to proceed with treatment.

There is no sense in going over the finances for a huge treatment plan if they tell you they can only afford $70 in monthly payments. This means when you are trying to go over finances, it should not sound like this:

"You have a crown and two fillings to do. Your insurance pays $1000 a year and you will have a $50 deductible. Your insurance only pays for about half of your crown and then they will pay 80% of your fillings. But they pay on a silver filling, so you will also have an upgrade fee. We require half at the first visit and half at the second visit. So your estimated portion is $1200. We also have this wonderful third party financing, so if you want to make interest-free payments you can pay $300 down, then you can pay $81 a month or you can pay $200 a month for six months. Would you like to schedule?"

And this is when the patients look at you like a deer in the headlights and say, *"I will go home and think about it."*

Trust me, most dentists and team members are nodding their heads laughing and telling me this is exactly what they do. How did I know this? Because I once had tried to communicate with patients this way and realized it didn't get patients to commit to anything all day.

When they tell you that they can afford $200 a month, you simply show a doable VISUAL payment plan. You can say, *"Oh, looks like you can do $194 a month for twenty-four months and we can help you eat healthier and give you the teeth that function like you want."* They tell me, *"Yes, I can do that,"* and bam! It's a "yes" and they are scheduled today.

We are still running a business and people must pay for the services they receive. Guys, it is very costly for a business to act like a bank, so unless you have an actual signed promissory note and gain interest off loaning your patients money, all patients should pay now. Please don't feel like it's mean or you are obligated to do what you did in the *good ole days*. Handshakes or promises to pay aren't guaranteed. When can anyone go anywhere and not pay for their services? This is all a mindset issue. How will patients value you if you don't? We are healthcare professionals and patients need your help.

Another tip is to show your team how to schedule to goal. Show them what a perfect day looks like. Make sure your software shows the daily production goals and how much is scheduled when they are looking at the daily and monthly production. Trust me, people love to see visual images of exactly what you want.

That means you need to physically set your monthly goal if you are going to enter a number into your software for the team to know where you stand. One way you can do that is to look at your best year's production, take the top three highest months, and find out your average. To figure out your average, add those top three months together, divide the sum by three, and that becomes the average monthly production that you know you can accomplish. If you feel ambitious or need to raise those numbers, then take the average you know you can do and raise that number by 15% to set a new monthly goal. Next, train the entire team on how to schedule to goal. I can physically show you all how if you need help.

Okay, doctors, I am sensing some of you may be resistant to this. Here may be your existing mindset: *"Heidi, I don't want them knowing how much I make!"* or *"Heidi, I don't want them to think that my financial numbers are more important than patient care."* Trust me, doctors, your employees are smart, and they assume a doctor is rich anyways. Help them follow a roadmap that prevents roller-coaster income.

Your Schedule and Income Need To Be Predictable

Make sure your team understands that the schedule is the top priority. This means if there is an opening in the schedule, it's all hands on deck to fill it. You can't waste time...time is money and if you don't fill the schedule, you will most likely experience roller-coaster income. People tend to get cranky when their income is inconsistent. Your patients want to be taken care of as soon as possible, and they are most likely more important than some of the menial tasks we are doing.

Let me help you by listing some ways you can minimize the open time in your schedule:

- *Have an ASAP or short call list at all times: run that report and offer an appointment.*
- *Look for emergency patients that need to be seen.*
- *Check for completed lab cases to deliver.*
- *Send a mass text out using a HIPAA-approved third party application and let patients know two dates and times that you have available.*
- *Look for overdue family members that can come with your scheduled patients.*
- *Run your unscheduled patient list and reactivate your patients who haven't completed treatment.*
- *Take time to use the intraoral camera on the existing patients who are already in your schedule and watch the results you get.*

Remember, one way that you can make a BIG IMPACT in your practice is to make sure all clinical team members are trained in taking intraoral photos and having discussions with patients.

If your case acceptance isn't where you want it to be, I need to ask you, *"Are you taking intraoral photos and doing that 100% on a consistent basis?"*

Another issue I see is that team members are unable to take photos as much as we would like them to. Let's solve that. Do you have an intraoral camera in every operatory readily available and one who person can fully function to snap a photo without needing someone else to assist them? Trust me, if you want results, this is definitely an area that you should invest in your dental practice.

You see, a picture is worth a thousand words. Dental offices that do that one step easily make an extra $10,000 more a month. Go ahead, try it consistently for a month and measure your results. If employees are trained on treatment case reviews, communication skills and how to share with patients what we see, then when the patient sees their areas of concern, patients will literally ask you to fix their teeth as soon as possible.

This area is truly where you have a gold mine in your office. #OverflowingTreasureChest

FREEDOM TO LIVE

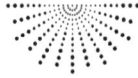

Unexpected Rewards

I did not grow up with a silver spoon in my mouth and we certainly didn't vacation like others. Traveling for our household meant taking a road trip with an ice chest packed with food. One day, I remember my dad bringing home a five-gallon glass water jug and telling us kids, *"Whatever money is in this jar by summer is what we will use to go on a family vacation."* This was super exciting for all of us as that jar looked really big. I was about six years old and I asked my parents, *"Where will the money come from?"* My dad reached in his pocket, grabbed the change, and dropped it into the jug. We all smiled. He said, *"Every time the store gives us back change, we will drop it in the jug."*

So, when my brother, sister and I went anywhere, we searched for change on the ground and brought it home to put in the jar. I loved the different sounds the coins made when we dropped them in. Sometimes, we even put our hard-earned "tooth fairy" money in the jar. Well, summer came and my parents gathered us around the table and told us the jar weighed twenty-seven pounds. I thought we were rich!!! My dad dumped the jar out as coins filled our kitchen table. He showed us his newly bought coin organizer and paper coin holders that we were told to stuff and he would bring to the bank. We all participated for hours, separating coins and stuffing envelopes. We anxiously waited to hear how much we saved and what we could afford to do on our family vacation.

The next day, my dad went to the bank and at dinner he told us we had $485. Now in 1976, we could do quite a bit with that. I will never forget our road trip to Universal Studios. We all knew how much effort it took all year to save for the trip. Dad told us that we would eat the food that Mom prepared in the ice chest and instructed us not to ask for anything else to buy while we were in the theme park. I also remember a homeless man asking for money and instead my mom provided him lunch.

At the end of the day, my parents thanked us for not begging for cotton candy or souvenirs and surprised us by telling us we could get ice cream waffle cones inside the theme park. It was one of my favorite family vacations.

I learned from a young age that the process of reaching a destination by working as a team involves setting goals with a deadline, anticipation, working together, some delayed gratification, charitable giving, abundance mentality, and if we maturely behaved, we received unexpected rewards. It's like you are earning jewels on your crown without even knowing it. Sometimes, I am teaching dentists and their teams concepts and later they realize the long-term benefits that they have gained for their practice and in their life.

> **You will get all you want in life,**
> **if you help enough other people**
> **get what they want.**
> **—Zig Ziglar**

I believe connections and relationships with your family, your community, your patients, and your team are the key to any successful business. I love training people in communication skills and team building to transform and elevate their work culture.

People love working as a team when everyone is rowing in the same direction! Be a leader, inspire others, establish accountability, and hire the right team. Having a happy, cohesive team is not just a fantasy; they actually exist when you have your foundation in place and when you are the captain of your ship.

If you'd like a team-building exercise to develop the expected character traits to minimize employee turnover, or being "fired" by an employee, contact me. Don't lose good employees over one bad apple. Value and protect each employee so you can make a bigger impact with your "dental family." Imagine the jewels you will earn with your positivity and encouragement.

The purpose of creating an A-team is to provide the framework that will increase your team's ability to creatively solve issues, thus allowing you to focus on your growing dental practice. When you have increased participation, it promotes more ownership of decisions, processes, and improvements.

It's time to focus on creating an engaged and aligned team. This is done by building relationships based on trust and respect from the inside out. Your goals need to be clear, concise, attainable, and written down.

Guys, it's time to get comfortable with the uncomfortable so you can excel at everything you want to do. If something isn't working, we need to do something differently. Part of having a clear business plan is to set a clear vision for the practice and decide who is doing what and by when. The first step is to discuss WHY you are doing what you are doing with your team. We must remember our "why" in every decision we make and not settle for less.

Insanity is doing the same thing over and over again and expecting different results.
—Albert Einstein

You do not have to do this alone! I am willing to be right by your side and help you. Let's do this together and we will all celebrate reaching your goals!

CALLING IN THE COAST GUARD TO CREATE BALANCE IN YOUR LIFE!

Count Your Marbles

One day I read the story of 1000 marbles and remember bawling my head off. The theory the story teaches us is about how the average person lives to about seventy-five years old which equals 3900 Saturdays. One day, I was rocking my one-month old baby girl, Julia, and realized that I only had 932 Saturdays before she turned eighteen years old. The story was emotional to me. The point is that it helped me gain perspective on my priorities.

Imagine I have two mason jars with marbles in them. Each marble represents years of my life. One jar has fifty marbles in it and the other has twenty-five. If every year I picked up a marble out of the jar of twenty-five and put it in the one that represented my age, could you imagine how scary it would look as the marbles diminished? Now, this is not to make you cry, it's to help you cherish your time here on earth. It is moments like these when I go hug my family and pick up the phone to call them to have meaningful conversations. Every moment you have is making decisions about your life.

As you may have noticed in my stories, our family started off with the bare minimum and we didn't complain. My dad taught us how to respect others, budget, work as a team, serve others in need, and be considerate and grateful. I believe the main traits I learned from him are to have faith, don't sweat things that won't matter a few years from now, and keep pressing forward.

Quitting is not an option when you have a destination to reach. As a little girl, I had big dreams and goals. Like my grandparents and my parents, I wanted to have my own great life. I dreamed of the perfect life; the wonderful home, the perfect family, and having fun all the time. I wanted all families to have more than enough. I saw how hard my family worked and wished life wasn't so difficult for them. As some of us discover, our dreams and goals can get shot down and reality sets in! Sometimes, we even lower our standards, settle for less, give up on our dreams, and feel as though we must not deserve more.

Others of us get sick and tired of being sick and tired and we take action. Did you know that your unconscious mind doesn't know the difference between the truth and a lie? That means we can reprogram our brains. Have you ever listened to your own self-talk?

I had a time in my life when I had to tell myself to stop self-loathing, say positive declarations...and dream again. I put on my captain's hat and said, *"I am starting my own company! Enough is enough and the bare minimum is not enough for me and my family!"*

Get this; I started telling some very successful dental colleagues about my business plan of being an international virtual dental consultant, thinking they would tell me how smart it was and thinking they would totally fire me up! Guess what? They didn't! Many said things like, *"That will never work!", "No one will pay you for that!"* and so forth.

I knew that I was not willing to live on an airplane and in hotels to be a traveling consultant and leave my family to make a living. After all, my dreams and goals were to spend *more* time with family and friends, not less! I borrowed some money and hired a business coach who listened to MY vision for MY life and helped me reverse engineer my vision with a clear business plan, and BAM! I ignore the naysayers, pressed forward, and now I am living the good life that I always dreamed of.

For about ten years, I ran a successful virtual consulting business.

Even when the COVID-19 pandemic hit in 2020 and dentists were shut down, I had all my systems in place so I could continue helping dentists and consultants all over the world. My schedule was full; I helped dental consultants redesign their business, donated time to struggling dentists, and worked with dozens of clients at one time. Even while working for free for some, it was a rewarding and record year for me.

Helping Others Bring Joy

Wanting to make a bigger impact in serving the dental community, even though I had minimal time to spare, I realized that I needed to write this book to help even more people. When you adjust your mindset, follow your heart, and take action on the calling for your life, you always live in abundance and improve your perception of how you see the world.

When others see your passion and authenticity, they are attracted to you, want to connect with you, and want to do business with you. I did have to make the choice (many times) to not let others hold me back from living life to the fullest. I knew I wanted more for my children and grandchildren than I had myself. Now that I am fifty and feeling a bit on the older side, I cherish every day that I wake up.

About nine years ago, when we discussed retirement, my husband, Dale, and I decided he would stop working while I continue to run my coaching practice. We began to dream about living on The Big Island of Hawaii and deep down wondered if we could actually do it.

We had many discussions about how we wanted retirement life to look, and we had fun setting some big audacious goals and dreaming about the good life. We wanted to move to Hawaii because we are happiest when we are in warmer weather and playing outdoors.

Each year we accomplished items on our checklist, met with our financial planner, talked with our coach, and even with a couple of setbacks, we kept pressing forward. We sacrificed, we saved, we planned, and prepared for our retirement life.

Was it easy? Nope. Was it worth it? Most definitely! Almost three years ago, my husband retired from being a chief of a fire department. Pulling the plug from a thirty year career is scary. For most men, they feel like they lose their identity, and it was a very scary decision to make. With ample coaching and financial planning, we decided to take the plunge and finalize more goals.

Another one of our top priorities was getting as healthy as possible and this truly drove our dream to live on an island. We knew in our core that we needed to live where we would enjoy the outdoor activities that we loved to do. When he retired, we bought our first home in Hawaii, and now we spend time kayaking, swimming, paddle boarding, scuba diving, hiking, cycling, eating island delish, hanging out with friends and family, barbequing all year, helping neighbors with their needs, shopping for island clothes, exploring, and watching sunsets from our own lanai.

Prior to living here, we passionately discussed what life would be like being able to go outdoors all year long. We accomplished our big audacious goal that we were not sure was even possible. I knew from how much we visited Hawaii and how much we talked about our dreams that we had to live there. Some date nights, we laughed about how MUCH we discussed our dreams and goals. We also wanted others to come visit and we would love to feel like we were giving people more vacations.

Now, I work during the day and enjoy island life afterward. As we started our "vacation anytime we choose" life, we felt so much joy. Living on a relaxed island, life was a huge dream come true. Our health improved immediately. Within two weeks, I no longer needed any allergy medications or an inhaler.

My husband, Dale, gained a couple of Ironman© coaches and started his training for triathlons. With the guidance, taking action, and tracking results he lost thirty-five pounds and he tells people, *"I am in better shape than I have been in thirty years!"* Keep your eye out for him becoming an official Ironman©. As a wife, I see a huge difference in him having more time to do the things he wants to do, and I really enjoy him even more each day. #HealthyLifeStyle

Was it easy? If it was easy, wouldn't everyone be living their ideal dream life? Did I actually think it was possible when we first started planning? Not really, but we did not allow any negative thinking, nor did we give attention to the what ifs, the nay-sayers, and the challenges that popped up.

To help with my success, I have a supportive coach at all times. When you find the right coach, they stretch you, encourage you, keep you focused, give you direction, and help you make better business decisions.

If you get to know me, you will discover that I share this with you to tell you that my dad was right. You CAN achieve anything you want. You just need to put the effort out to accomplish it. I want to help each and every one of you to live the life you choose to live. After all, who doesn't want a great story to tell?

People ask me all the time, *"What made you become a coach?"* Honestly, it took my dad's death to take the leap of faith to start my own company. I kept hearing his voice telling me that I was smart enough to become a successful entrepreneur. My reason that I became a dental business coach was because I realized if I worked for one dentist, coached in my community in my spare time, or taught a group of dentists in a study club that I couldn't help as many as I wanted to or make as big of a splash in the world. By being an international dental coach, a guest on podcasts, a speaker, and an author, I help hundreds of dentists and their teams to be less stressed, work smarter, and hopefully live longer.

Let's face it, people who work too hard tend to develop health problems, and even worse, die younger than they should. I don't want anyone to go through the grief that I did! Most people may be thinking, *I already know this.* Yep, it's human nature to not do anything with that knowledge. That is why the accountability piece is so important. My clients love to follow the steps and achieve more with me by their side.

We have all heard that knowledge is power and to keep learning. The real power is the application of this knowledge. I help my clients apply it to succeed. You and only you can decide how much effort you will put forth to satisfy your burning desires. It's time to say, *"I'm willing to do more and I deserve it!"*

> **The cave that you fear to enter**
> **holds the treasure that you seek.**
> **—Joseph Campbell**

Now What?

Here we are at the end of this book. While the book is ending, our journey is just beginning. Here are the next steps I advise you to take:

- Take better and smarter actions; set goals you REALLY want. As a coach, I help you distinguish between what you coulda, shoulda, oughta. I will enable you to identify what lies deep down in your heart and will inspire you to take action...which will give you a healthier outcome.

- I help with what needs to be done in order to move to the next step. My goal is to help you operate from the "present," right where you are at, and plan for your future. In other words, together, we will develop better answers and solve the issues that hold you back from a balanced life. Let's raise the bar, level up your business, and build your confidence.

- Create room by scheduling time to develop good practices. When you take these actions, your business and personal growth will accelerate.

- Best of all, we work on a clear, written business plan, see projects to completion, make key decisions, prioritize, train, increase collections, and launch your business forward.

- This book is to help you and trust me, it's best to take some action. I want you to write down your top five biggest takeaways in your journal.

Listen, if you schedule a call with me and hire me as a coach, I will make you this promise: I will give you a full living brochure and a comprehensive practice analysis so you know exactly where you stand, and then we'll develop a clear business plan. This is the foundation for true success. What do you say, Doc? That's HUGE! #PeaceOfMindIsPriceless

I recommend that you reserve a consultation with me. Here is how: go to CoachHeidiMount.com/practice-analysis/ and when you are in front of your dental practice software, fill out the confidential web form. Then, schedule your face-to-face call with me on my website.

You may be asking yourself, *I've got these steps now to take. Why would I want to work with a coach?* The answer is that you receive high level coaching. When you get my eyes on your practice, I help you and your team find the missing revenue in your dental practice, improve your systems, set better goals, and then guide you on how to reach those goals. This is not me telling you how to run your practice; I work with you as the CEO and your team to level up your business. #WorkLifeBalance

We all need a vision to give ourselves something worth doing. Together, with the dentist at the helm and with me mapping the vision, my clients do more than they would have done on their own. My expertise helps you focus better so you can produce results more quickly. I provide my clients with the life experiences, business brain, time-saving resources, tools, support, and structure to accomplish more. People hire me because they want more and they want it easy to do. They love adding me to their team, bragging about what they did, and inviting me to celebrate with them.

When my clients hire me, they take themselves more seriously, they take more effective and focused actions, they stop putting up with the things that are holding them back, they create momentum, and they set better goals for what THEY want. They are no longer throwing spaghetti at a wall trying to see what will stick. We set up a clear business foundation for success.

How is this done? Well, we meet for focused coaching sessions and it's as if you have an I.V. to the coach. Yes, I am right by your side guiding you and relieving weight off your shoulder. I help remove the confusion out of the decisions you have to make. It's very important to know the big picture even if you are doing very well. Are you going to be financially independent or retire early enough? Is your dental practice valuable to a buyer or leaving you a legacy? *"Heidi, I don't know what I don't know..."* You and so many other docs...don't worry, I help with this process.

The only difference between successful people and those who are not are HABITS. I help you identify your motivation and guide you in the decision-making process.

No one knows how many summers, vacations, trips, or days we have to live. It's time to take care of YOU and make sure you can make a big splash in this world, too.

Life is not about the number of destinations you have been to, it's about the number of journeys you have experienced. I want you to enjoy your journey, loved ones, and most importantly, your health.

From the bottom of my heart, I wish you the very best Bon Voyage and as we say on the Hawaiian Islands,

"A hui hou (until we meet again)!"

Heidi Mount

ACKNOWLEDGMENTS

I have to start by thanking my husband Dale Mount. He is truly my rock, my support system, and my ironman. Having an entrepreneurial wife takes a tremendous amount of understanding and lots of help. You are truly my superman and I feel so honored to be married to you. I look forward to growing old with you. Oh, and I always smile inside when you tell me, *"As you wish."* Thank you for tremendously enhancing my life.

Dear Julia Mount, my amazing daughter, I'm grateful you supported our decision to live in Hawaii even though it is across the ocean. You put my passion for island life above your own needs and I am so thankful for you. There is not a day that goes by that I don't miss being in the same town. When you were born, you were not breathing and you fought to live. And now you are the strongest woman in my life. I am truly honored to be your mom. Your independence, determination, creativity, and boldness will keep you conquering this world and reaching your own dreams and goals. I love you from the beach and back.

To my sister, Wendy Herbert, you have always been by my side. Thank you for being the most understanding friend and helpful sister that I could ever ask for. I pray that your daughters and your life are truly blessed more than you could ever imagine. I look forward to us being crazy old ladies together.

My dearest Debbie Treese, thank you for always being there for me and being a part of our family. I can't put into words how much I appreciate all your positivity, quality time you spend with me, and our cherished memories together. You have literally worked by my side, joined me in devotions, prayed with me, kept me level-headed, shown me so much abundant love, encouraged me, and truly listened any time I needed you. You are the one who knows how to make me smile from the inside out.

To my scuba instructor who held my hand on my first dive, Steve Mills, and his amazing wife, Sarah Mills, thank you for rescuing me from being "houseless" and for all of your support. Through you, I met the love of my life, Dale. I am ever so grateful that you introduced us to scuba diving and sparked our dream of someday living in Hawaii. You opened many doors for me, and I am so appreciative and honored to be a part of the Mills family. And I am grateful for all you have done to take care of my family as well. You both have true servant hearts, ones that this world is so lucky to know and experience.

Dr. Ron Arndt, I have felt so blessed that you came into my life at 46 years old. You are truly like a dad, mentor, and teacher to me. You have taught me advanced financial and retirement planning, and you have given me so many resources and tools to be a very impactful dental coach. I am honored that you have included me in your family and opened your home up to me. Thank you for having so many traits of my father; your sacrificial love makes me cry. I am truly honored to know you and to call you friend.

Marilee Sears...giiiiirrrrrrlllll, you know what you did for me! You are a true friend and inspiration to everyone with whom you come into contact. Our lives were parallel in so many ways that we have a special divine connection. Thank you from the bottom of my heart for including my family and me in your life. I love our girl time together and how we hold each other accountable.

Jane Powers, I'm grateful Marilee was sitting next to me and encouraged me to go to your breakout room at the conference. She said, *"You're absolutely terrified to speak on stage! It sounds like you should be in the 'Speak With Authority Conference'!"* You held my hand and said, *"Girlfriend, you're going to get over this fear and I'm going to help you!"* And you did. Thank you for giving me exactly what I needed with your customized coaching.

To all of you who impacted my life with your kindness, I can't say thank you enough! From the bottom of my heart, thank you friends, colleagues, and family. Because of you, I am an author with stories and experiences to share with the world. My heart's desire is to impact someone's life as you have mine.

REFERENCES

Chapter 1

Jack's Diving Locker has the registered copyright for Pelagic Magic ©.

Baron, Barbara. 20Quotes.com. https://20quotes.com/authors/barbara-baron

Tzu, Lao, 1986 January-February, *Yoga Journal*, Number 66, Bodywork: "Choosing an Approach to Suit Your Needs" by Joseph Heller and William A. Henkin, Start Page 28, Quote Page 56, Published by Active Interest Media, Inc., Boulder, Colorado. (Google Books Preview)

Sparks, Nicholas. Goodreads. https://www.goodreads.com/quotes/314001-to-all-the-ships-at-sea-and-all-the-ports

Chapter 2

"A Quote by Martin Luther King, Jr." Goodreads. https://www.goodreads.com/quotes/16312-faith-is-taking-the-first-step-even-when-you-can-t

Burg, Bob. Endless Referrals: Network Your Everyday Contacts into Sales. New York: McGraw Hill, 2006.

"A Quote by Henry Ford." Goodreads. https://www.goodreads.com/quotes/7482-you-can-t-build-a-reputation-on-what-you-are-going.

"A Quote by Andre Gide." Goodreads. https://www.goodreads.com/quotes/4661-man-cannot-discover-new-oceans-unless-he-has-the-courage

"Quote by Irene C. Kassorla." Goodreads. https://www.goodreads.com/quotes/413810-you-must-have-control-of-the-authorship-o-your-own

John Shedd 2006, The Yale Book of Quotations by Fred R. Shapiro, Section: John A. Shedd, Page 705, Yale University Press, New Haven.

Chapter 3:

"Capable Quotes." AZ Quotes. Holtz, Lou. https://www.azquotes.com/quotes/topics/capable.html.

"Quote by Stuart Scott." Goodreads. https://www.goodreads.com/quotes/5461349-don-t-downgrade-your-dream-just-to-fit-your-reality-upgrade

"Quote by Henry Ford." Goodreads. https://www.goodreads.com/quotes/978-whether-you-think-you-can-or-you-think-you-can-t-you-re

Chapter 5:

New United Motors is trademarked and owned by <u>NEW UNITED MOTOR MANUFACTURING, INC.</u>

Toyota is trademarked and owned by <u>TOYOTA JIDOSHA KABUSHIKI KAISHA.</u>

General Motors is trademarked and owned by <u>GENERAL MOTORS LLC.</u>

"Stephen Covey Quote: Always treat your employees exactly as you want them to treat your best customers." AZ Quotes. https://www.azquotes.com/quote/1078705

"Quote by John C. Maxwell." Goodreads. https://www.goodreads.com/quotes/273744-leaders-must-be-close-enough-to-relate-to-others-but

Chapter 6:

"Stephen Covey Quote: Live your life by a compass, not a clock." AZ Quotes. https://www.azquotes.com/quote/868461

"Arthur Schopenhauer Quote." Quote Fancy. https://quotefancy.com/quote/768387/Arthur-Schopenhauer-The-common-man-is-not-concerned-about-the-passage-of-time-the-man-of

Chapter 7

Carlisle, Bob. *A Journal of Butterfly Kisses.* W Pub Group, October 1, 1997.

The Energizer Bunny is trademarked and owned by Energizer Brands, LLC.

Chapter 8:

Nightingale, Earl. Your Grass is Greener. Nightingale Legacy, 2019.

Chapter 9:

Universal Studios is trademarked and owned by UNIVERSAL CITY STUDIOS LLC.

Ziglar, Zig. *Great Quotes from Zig Ziglar: 250 Inspiring Quotes from the Master Motivator and Friends.* New York: Gramercy Books, 1997.

"Insanity Is Doing the Same Thing Over and Over Again and Expecting Different Results." Quote Investigator, September 7, 2019. https://quoteinvestigator.com/tag/al-anon/.

Chapter 10:

Davis, Jeffrey. *1,000 Marbles: A Little Something About Precious Time.* Andrews McMeel Publishing, June 15, 2001.

"Ironman" is copyrighted, trademarked and owned by the World Triathlon Corporation.

"Joseph Campbell." genordell.com. https://www.genordell.com/stores/maison/JosephCampbell.htm.

INDEX

www.ingramcontent.com/pod-product-compliance
Lightning Source LLC
Chambersburg PA
CBHW070658190326
41458CB00053B/6924/J